Montjuïc

introduction

Disseny - 'design' is the defining characteristic of Barcelona, a city at once provincial and cosmopolitan, bourgeois and avant-garde, compact, yet immensely rich and diverse: a national capital without a country. From the improbable architecture of Gaudí and his contemporaries, to the slick shops and bars which cram both the Old City and the newer Eixample, Barcelona presents an engaging sophistication which few larger cities can rival. With its galleries, museums, restaurants and clubs, it is a cultural banquet at which its citizens feast with gusto and welcome all as guests.

This book is intended to guide you through the myriad sights of this flamboyant city; to help you enjoy the best food, the most exciting night-life and the best shopping it has to offer. It is arranged thematically into four art areas, each taking in a different aspect of the city's culture, be it the vision of the Modernists, the singular art of medieval Catalonia, the genius of Picasso, or the latest in contemporary creations.

Barcelona's Eixample, laid out in the late-1800s, for the successful Catalan middle and upper classes, was the playground of a series of revolutionary architects whose Art Nouveau stylings came to characterize the city. The most famous, Antoni Gaudí, created La Sagrada Família, whose towering spires are a symbol of Barcelona. To the south, the Picasso Museum reigns over La Ribera, a medieval neighbourhood whose narrow streets are surrounded by the sturdy stone walls of the palaces built for the nobility and wealthy burghers. Rising above the town, Montjuic is Barcelona's triumphant salute to the 20th century, a suburb of museums and gardens raised in the 1920s and capped in the 1990s by the Olympic installations. In its shadow, the Raval, another medieval neighbourhood, has been shaking itself out of centuries of decay and re-emerging as a hot-bed of the cutting-edge, epitomized by the MACBA, the contemporary art museum at its core.

GAUDÍ AND
THE EIXAMPLE

When Barcelona shook off five centuries of lethargy and depression and emerged in the mid-19c as a centre of trade and industry, its boom in prosperity coincided with the blossoming of Modernisme, the style of art and architecture also known as Art Nouveau. A perfect style for the city's conservative yet cultured bourgeoisie, Modernisme was at once daring in terms of forms and media but cautious in its emphasis on the decorative. In Barcelona there was also a nationalist dimension in the extent to which the Gothic style from Catalonia's medieval golden age influenced the development of Modernisme. When the city spread beyond its medieval confines with the laying out of the new city, the Eixample, and the bucolic suburbs of Pedralbes and beyond, it was designed very much as a Modernista city. By the early 20c, when both the artistic movement and the city's expansion had slowed down, the result was an oddly homogenous and strikingly beautiful cityscape.

The three major figures of the Modernista movement were the architects Antoni Gaudí, Lluís Domènech i Montaner and Josep Puig i Cadafalch. Most of their works are found in new Barcelona, although important early Modernista constructions can be found in the Old City.

EIXAMPLE

In the mid-19c Barcelona was still largely confined to the area within its 14c town walls, but it had reached bursting point. The plan for expanding the city that was eventually accepted, in the face of considerable opposition, was that of Ildefons Cerdà, who proposed a regular grid of blocks (*mansanes* or *illes*), each of which incorporated shops, apartments and garden courtyards. As the streets were laid, the upper and middle classes left the old town for their new, more spacious homes. Although the garden courtyards were soon swallowed up by warehouse and factory spaces, the basic plan survived until recent rises in the value of real estate began to force some residents out. The traditional configuration in the Eixample's blocks featured shops on the ground floor, the wealthy living on the first floor, with the less affluent occupying spaces higher up. The Eixample is a splendid area for strolling: its building are a dizzying spectacle and its galleries, shops and restaurants provide frequent opportunities for diversion and refreshment.

La Sagrada Família

OPEN	Oct-March, Mon-Sun 9.00-18.00; April-Sept, Mon-Sun 9.00-20.00. 25-26/12 and 6/1 10.00-14.00
CLOSED	1/1 and 6/1
CHARGES	€8; reduced admission €5; with guided tour €11; lift €2; audioguide €3 Reduced admission for students. Ruta del Modernisme, Barcelona Card and Bus Turístic discounts
TELEPHONE	932 073 031
WWW.	sagradafamilia.org
MAIN ENTRANCE	Plaça de la Sagrada Família

DISABLED ACCESS	Yes
METRO	Sagrada Família
SHOP	Books about Gaudí and Barcelona. Wide range of Gaudí-related souvenirs includes posters, T-shirts, jewellery and stationery

Guided tours in English: Nov-March, Fri, Sat, Sun and Mon at 11.00 and 13.00. April-Oct, Mon-Sun at 11.00, 13.00, 15.00 and 17.30 (at 17.00 in Oct).

La Sagrada Família Towers

The Temple Expiatori de la Sagrada Família was originally planned as a church to house a copy of the Holy House of Loreto, one of Catholic Italy's most revered shrines, an idea put forward by Josep Maria Bocabella, the founder of a religious society devoted to the cult of St Joseph. Building work began in 1882 under the direction of Francesc de Paula de Villar, but disagreements with Bocabella led to his dismissal after only a small section of the crypt had been completed. On 3 October 1883, the task of completing the building was entrusted to the 31-year-old Antoni Gaudí, who developed a plan of ever-increasing originality, ambitiousness and scale. While respecting the Gothic cathedral plan of ambulatory, transepts and five aisles, he intended the building to be 60 metres wide at the crossing and have a central nave 95 metres long.

Gaudí was involved in the construction of the building for the rest of his life, refusing to take on any other architectural commissions after the death in 1914 of his close friend and collaborator, Francesc Berenguer i Mestres. He lived in a shack on the site, but was not destitute, as was believed until recently. He had just become so absorbed in his work that he was totally uninterested in material things and chose to live a frugal life. At the time of Gaudí's death, in 1926, all that had been completed of the building was the crypt, the apse and part of the Nativity façade. It narrowly escaped demolition at the hands of the anarchists during the Civil War.

Work on the building was renewed in 1952 and has been continuing ever since. It might be possible to complete the building by 2015, though there are many people who believe that the place should have been left as a monumental shell commemorating Gaudí's visionary but wayward genius.

Antoni Gaudí (1852–1926)

Born in Reus (near Tarragona), Antoni Gaudí is the most famous of the Modernista architects and the greatest influence on the look of Barcelona today. In 1878, he qualified as an architect. Elies Rogent, director of the Barcelona College of Architecture, said at that time: 'We've given our diploma to a madman or a genius: time will tell us which one he is'. Gaudí assisted on the installations at the Parc de la Ciutadella and on various other minor projects around the old city. By 1883 he was well established and had been awarded commissions for public, civil and church projects around the peninsula, but especially in Barcelona, thanks to the patronage of the powerful industrialist Eusebi Güell. During this period he drew heavily on neo-Gothic, Moorish and Mudéjar elements for both the structure and detail of his buildings. By 1900 he had developed his own style, which tended towards the abstract but was based on organic and geometric forms, as can be seen at La Pedrera, Casa Battló and Park Güell. From 1917 until his death, he concentrated solely on La Sagrada Família, the culmination of his technical and imaginative development.

Gaudí was a pious Catholic and a detail-obsessed artist. Endeavouring to control every aspect of his creative work, he mastered techniques such as metal and woodwork and glass-blowing so that he could better direct the artisans working under him. His technical innovations included *trencadís*, decorative work in ceramic, similar to mosaic, and the catenary arch, created by suspending a rope or chain between two points and then inverting the resulting arc. After Gaudí died, struck by a tram, the unfinished Sagrada Família languished, before work was resumed under public subscription later in the century. Gaudí's work continues to excite passion and argument. His most faithful supporters have undertaken to have him beatified, the initial step on the road to Catholic sainthood.

PASSION FAÇADE Entering from the Plaça de la Sagrada Família, the Passion façade looms up before you, with six columns that resemble elongated bones. It was begun in 1954, based on Gaudí's plans, and the four bell-towers were completed in 1976. The stark geometric sculptural decoration was executed by Josep Maria Subirachs and represents the Passion and Death of Christ, as Gaudí had intended. The three doors are dedicated to the Christian virtues.

You can take a lift part of the way up the towers, then walk up the spiral steps inside the openwork spires, a surreal experience likely to induce claustrophobia, agoraphobia and vertigo, all at the same time. Look out for the stone snakes, lizards and frogs, thought to symbolize the banishment of evil from the church. The lollipop-like tips of the towers, which are covered in Murano glass, represent bishops, and are decorated with the cross, mitre, ring and scales. Each tower is devoted to one of the twelve apostles, with their initials inscribed in the golden cross at the top.

MUSEUM Located to the right of the main entrance, the displays chart the conception and implementation of the project. Photographs show the development of the construction process and there are also models of various parts of the structure, plans of the ongoing work and information about Gaudí's main collaborators. Exhibits explain how Gaudí worked out how to build his beloved parabolic arches, hanging chains loosely between two points to see how the curve formed. A model shows how he used this technique to devise the structure of the church for the Colonia Güell.

La Sagrada Família Passion façade

La Sagrada Família Nativity façade

NATIVITY FAÇADE The dynamic, sculptural façade, dedicated to the Nativity of Christ, was built between 1891 and 1900 using stone from the quarries at Montjuïc. It features three portals in the shape of parabolic arches, representing, from left to right, Hope, Charity and Faith. These are encrusted with a mass of figures, some made from life casts. The largest is the central **Charity portal**, which features the Coronation of the Virgin Mary, the birth of Jesus and the Adoration of the Shepherds and the Wise Men. Angels play musical instruments and a pelican is about to take flight. A snake bearing an apple is coiled around a palm tree, representing the Garden of Eden. Turtles are embedded in the base of the columns, symbolizing longevity and the continued existence of the Church. The portal is crowned by a painted ceramic cypress tree adorned with doves. The decoration on the **Faith portal** includes the Presentation of Christ in the Temple, while the Hope portal features the Flight to Egypt and the Massacre of the Innocents.

The strange oozing forms surrounding the figures give a grotto-like character to the portals, which accords well with the tapering crenellated towers above, the shape of which was inspired by the curiously eroded peaks behind the monastery at Montserrat. These mountains are one of the most potent symbols of Catalunya and would have been very important to Gaudí. When he died, only one of the towers had been built, but the other three were erected soon afterwards by Domènech Sugrañes. There is another lift here to take you part of the way up the towers.

NAVE Construction is in full swing in the nave, where the columns sprout branches just like trees and the brick vault is decorated with palm leaves and hyperboloid forms. The columns in the transept are made of porphyry from Iran. The six domes being built are devoted to the four Evangelists, the Virgin Mary and Jesus Christ. The last of these is the biggest, rising to a height of 170 metres and crowned with a cross.

APSE Facing C/Provença, the neo-Gothic structure was completed under Gaudí's direction in 1893 and features

La Sagrada Família Nave

naturalistic motifs, with gargoyles of frogs, snakes and lizards. The pinnacles are adorned with wheat, which represents the Eucharist. Inside, there are seven polygonal chapels and an ambulatory around the presbytery.

CRYPT A staircase to the left of the apse leads down to the crypt. Extensively damaged during the Civil War, it was restored by Francesc Quintana in 1940. The circular neo-Gothic structure has a ribbed vault and and an ambulatory containing seven chapels. Gaudí is buried in the chapel of Our Lady of Carmen. His tomb is covered by a simple stone inscribed with his place of birth, Reus, and his position as the architect of the Sagrada Família. A relief of the *Holy Family* by Josep Llimona presides over the main altar.

ROSE CHAPEL Between the Nativity façade and the apse, this chapel on the corner of the cloister was designed by Gaudí and features rich decoration in Flamboyant Gothic style. The Madonna of the Rose is set within a pointed arch and flanked by St Dominic and St Catherine of Siena. Reliefs depict the dangers of temptation, with a woman being offered a bag of money by a monster in the form of a fish.

GLORY FAÇADE Work is pressing ahead on this façade, facing C/Mallorca, which will be the main entrance to the Cathedral. Devoted to the Glory of Jesus, the portal is adorned with palm trees and has 21 columns and 11 doors, with four bell-towers rising above.

SCHOOLS Immediately to the right of the visitor entrance is a reconstruction of the parish schools originally built in 1909-10. The wavy roof and walls enabled Gaudí to achieve maximum resistance using a minimum of materials. The building houses a permanent exhibition about Gaudí's workshop, which was originally situated within the site on the corner of C/Sardenya and C/Provenza. His desk has been recreated, and models and diagrams explain how he incorporated parabolic and helix-based forms into his designs.

HOSPITAL DE LA SANTA CREU I SANT PAU

OPEN	Tues & Sun 10.00-14.00, 50-minute guided tours (in English) every half hour
CLOSED	Always open for public access
CHARGES	€4.20; reduced admission for senior citizens and students Free guided tour with Route del Modernisme voucher
TELEPHONE	**932 919 484**
MAIN ENTRANCE	North end of Avinguda Gaudí
METRO	Hospital de Sant Pau

The Hospital is best visited on one of the guided tours, but as it is a functioning public building you are free to wander into the main hall and around the buildings of the 'garden' campus.

In many ways the squat expanse of the Hospital de la Santa Creu i Sant Pau is the antithesis of the vertical élan of Sagrada Família which towers at the opposite end of Avinguda Gaudí. It is Domènech i Montaner's practical and secular response to his great rival's work of spirituality and piety.

The city's main hospital had previously been the Hospital de la Santa Creu in the Raval (p 100), founded in 1401. When it was decided to build a modern facility for the Eixample, Domènech i Montaner was recruited and enlisted the collaboration of Pau Gargallo, Eusebi Arnau and other Modernista designers. It was designed in 1901 and took until 1930 to complete; after the architect's death in 1912 his son Pere carried on the work.

The main entry at the end of Avinguda Gaudí is pure Domènech i Montaner, an obvious homage to the Middle Ages, crowned by his trademark tower, here graced by clock. The entry hall has a dome supported by Gothic arches executed in the finest Art Nouveau style, in white and cream with gilt decoration.

Through the doors opposite the main entrance you reach the campus of the 'garden hospital', modelled on contemporary buildings in France, whose peaceful and airy atmosphere was believed to be conducive to recovery. The 48 pavilions, each an exceptional work of Modernista design, are arranged along two axial avenues; the architect also connected them with underground passages so that patients would not have to suffer inclement weather when moving around. The colourful exterior, with its carving, ironwork and irridescent glazed tiles, might be thought to convey a health-promoting optimism and contrast pleasingly with the traditional Catalan red-brick walls.

Picasso painted **Dead Woman** (1903) at the hospital, which is now on view in the Picasso Museum. Ironically, it was here – in his rival's creation – that Antoni Gaudí spent the last painful days of his life, after being struck down by a street car in 1926.

CASA MACAYA

OPEN	Mon–Fri 9.30–20.00; Sat 10.30–19.30, Sun 10.30–14.30
CHARGES	€6.50
TELEPHONE	**932 126 050**
MAIN ENTRANCE	Passeig de Sant Joan 108
METRO	Verdaguer

Ten minutes' walk west of La Sagrada Família stands Casa Macaya (1901), a stunning building by Josep Puig i Cadalfach, both Gaudí's and Domènech i Muntaner's colleague and rival. Puig i Cadalfach was a fervent Catalanist, and his designs draw heavily on 11c and 12c Romanesque, an artistic style considered characteristic of Catalonia formative's period as an independent, fully European nation. It was designed as a home for the businessman Roman Macaya. In contrast with Casa Amatller (p 24), also by Puig i Cadalfach, the façade of Casa Macaya is stark and smooth, except for the elaborate window and door decorations.

Inside, a voluminous entry hall gives way to neo-Moorish stylings, before a spectacular spiral staircase with touches of neo-Gothic masonry is reached. Remodelling has deprived the rest of the house of its origial décor. The Casa Macaya is currently the temporary home of the Museu de Ciencias (Science Museum). Over the door of the main entrance look for the carved bicycle, a friendly reference by the sculptor Arnau to Puig i Cadalfach's favourite mode of transport.

La Pedrera

OPEN	Mon-Sun 10.00-20.00
CLOSED	1/1, 6/1, 25-26/12
CHARGES	€6 full price; €3 reduced price for students and senior citizens Included on Articket, Ruta del Modernisme, Bus Turístic and Barcelona Card discount. Audioguide €3
TELEPHONE	**902 400 973**
WWW.	**caixacatalunya.es**
MAIN ENTRANCE	Passeig de Gràcia 92, corner of C/Provença
METRO	Diagonal
DIABLED ACCESS	Yes
SHOP	Good range of Gaudí-related gifts, including stationery, T-shirts and ceramics. Books on Gaudí, architecture and Barcelona. Jewellery inspired by La Pedrera by Chelo Sastre and other renowned designers
EATING	A small café on the ground floor and a bar on the roof terrace which is open July-Sept, daily 21.00-24.00, with live music

There are guided tours Mon-Fri at 18.00, Sat, Sun and PH at 11.00. Temporary exhibitions are held on the first floor.

La Pedrera was built in 1906-12 as a residential and commercial block commissioned by the local businessman Pere Milà i Roser Segimon. The massive curving façade is made of Montjuïc limestone which was sculpted into shape here on site. It is often compared to an abandoned quarry-face, which is why the building is usually known as La Pedrera, which means 'the Quarry', rather than its real name, the Casa Milà. The rippling and smoothly eroded forms are also reminiscent of waves, an image reinforced by the extraordinary recycled ironwork balconies by Josep Maria Jujol, which make the building look as if it has been strewn with seaweed. Some people think it resembles the Prades mountains, near where Gaudí was born. The originality of the building extends to the complex arrangement of the interior, which is centred around two undulating and irregular courtyards adorned with ceramics and traces of murals. The walls in the apartments curve too, with no sharp angles. There is an underground parking area, originally for cars and carriages, which is accessed by ramps and was highly innovative at the time. Most of the building is still residential apartments.

The Caixa de Catalunya Foundation bought La Pedrera in 1986 and restored and remodelled the sections now open to the public. These areas are at the top of the building and comprise informative displays charting Gaudí's career, the spectacular roof terrace, an apartment furnished in the style of the turn of the 20c and exhibits illustrating the changes taking place in Barcelona at that time.

ESPAI GAUDÍ A lift takes you up to the Espai Gaudí exhibition space in the attic. This space and the roof terrace were restored and remodelled in 1991-6 by Francisco Javier Asarta and Robert Brufau, under the direction of Enric Mira and advised by the art and architecture historian Raquel Lacuesta. The displays chart

La Pedrera Roof terrace

Gaudí's life and career in an informative and original way, from his earliest projects to the Sagrada Família, documented by photographs, plans, drawings, charts and audiovisuals. Models show how he created his trademark catenary arches and how he managed to make such good use of natural light. The exhibition provides an excellent introduction to Gaudí's work.

ROOF TERRACE The fantastical rooftop features strange twisted chimneys and ventilation shafts, coated with fragments of pottery, marble and glass. The straight and undecorated chimneys were later additions, as were the safety railings. Gaudí was reluctant to install railings, believing that these detracted from the wild mountain-top character of the roofline.

He had originally intended to add a sculptural group to this surrealistic landscape. More than four metres high, this would have represented either the Virgin of La Gràcia (the name of the former township which began at the Carrer de Provença) or the Virgin of Roser (in honour of his patron's wife). Milà, however, in view of the anarchist disturbances of the time, thought it unwise to crown the building with such a prominent Catholic symbol, and Gaudí had to content himself with the cross-like shape of the central chimney. From the roof there are panoramic views of the city from Tibidabo mountain down to the sea.

PEDRERA APARTMENT AND BARCELONA 1905-29 EXHIBITION
A staircase leads down to the Pedrera Apartment, where an exhibition shows how the city, society and industry were developing in the years Gaudí was working on his various projects in Barcelona. The apartment retains many original features and is decorated and furnished in the typical style of a middle-class family in the early 20c, complete with everyday objects, household utensils and children's toys. The bedroom furniture is by Gaspar Homar.

Mansana de la Discòrdia

Down the street from La Pedrera, the Mansana de la Discòrdia (the 'block of Discord') is one of the most photographed sites in the city. Here, on the same stretch of street, the three great Modernista architects worked in direct competition; each had been commissioned by a wealthy family to create a distinctive home in a frenzy of artistic and social one-upmanship. The most flamboyant is Gaudí's Casa Batlló, which will be the first building you encounter; next door is Puig i Cadalfach's more restrained Casa Amatller; and finally, at the far corner, Domènech i Montaner's exuberant Casa Lleó i Morera. Together the three buildings form one of the city's most original and striking architectural developments.

Mansana de la Discòrdia

CASA BATLLÓ

OPEN	There are plans to close it to the public, but call to confirm
TELEPHONE	932 160 306
WWW.	casabatllo.es
MAIN ENTRANCE	Passeig de Gràcia 43
METRO	Passeig de Gràcia

Gaudí worked on the Casa Batlló between 1904 and 1906, remodelling and extending an existing structure to create a family home for the textile baron Josep Batlló, a few of whose lucky descendants still live on the third floor.

The main façade bears out Gaudí's love of melting amorphous forms. It is encrusted with sparkly ceramic decorations like strange subaqueous forms made by his usual collaborator Josep Maria Jujol. The balconies resemble skulls, masks or perhaps sharks' teeth. The undulating, ceramic-tiled roof was almost certainly intended to suggest the figures of St George and the Dragon. The saint is represented by the turret crowned by a cross, and the dragon is evoked through ceramic tiles and ribs that appear to be the animal's scales and bones. The rear façade is much more sober, though it does have a colourful upper level resplendent with ceramic floral decorations. If the building is closed to the

Casa Batlló Façade

public, you can see it from an alley leading off the adjacent C/Aragó; or go into Servicio Estación, a DIY shop at C/Aragó 270, and make for the second floor, where there is a good view.

Casa Batlló Roof

The hall is a weird, underwater world where tapering, billowing walls are painted in cool shades of blue and grey. A staircase with a handrail like the curving backbone of some long-extinct monster leads upstairs to a room with a mushroom-shaped fireplace: couples used to sit on one side of it, with the girl's companion on the other. A skylight in the corner of the room lets the sun in to an otherwise dark space.

There are slats in the doors between the hall and the main salon, as Gaudí was a fervent advocate of ventilation. The amorphous stained-glass shapes on the doors are pale blue and lilac on the hall side, but change to mauve, terracotta and pewter on the other side. In the drawing room, the stained-glass windows overlooking the street feature pink and gold blobs, like exotic jellyfish. An inner courtyard, which in most apartment blocks would be an ugly, gloomy space, has been transformed by the use of shiny tiles, the colour gradually changing from the palest blue at ground level to vibrant cobalt at the top, creating the illusion of light at the darkest point.

CASA AMATLLER

OPEN	Mon–Fri 10.00–21.00, Sun 10.00-14.00
CHARGES	Admission free
TELEPHONE	**934 880 139**
MAIN ENTRANCE	Passeig de Gràcia 41
METRO	Passeig de Gràcia

Antoni Amatller had made his fortune as a chocolatier so the gingerbread house appearance of his home, by Puig i Cadalfach, is very appropriate. Casa Amatller (1898-1900) was the first of the three buildings of the *mansana* to be renovated (all were remodellings of pre-existing buildings). The main façade is an

Casa Amatller Façade

exercise in frenetic yet harmonious decoration, involving a range of materials including marble, wood, stone and ironwork, a pastiche of styles in which the architect's penchant for linking Catalonia to Europe, in this case northern Europe, is obvious (e.g. in the huge stepped gable). The sculptors Eusebi Arnau and Alfons Jujol helped to make the architect's vision a physical reality. Inside, you can view the entry hall and staircase, as well as the creaky old lift, which still works. Take note of the elegant bronze lamps and look up through the stairwell to the stained-glass dome which filters the light. Today the house is home to the **Bagués jewellery shop** as well as the **Centre del Modernisme**, a

Casa Amatller Gable

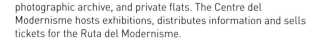

photographic archive, and private flats. The Centre del Modernisme hosts exhibitions, distributes information and sells tickets for the Ruta del Modernisme.

CASA LLEÓ MORERA

OPEN	Interior closed to public
MAIN ENTRANCE	Passeig de Gràcia 35
METRO	Passeig de Gràcia

Domènech i Montaner's Casa Lleó Morera (1902-6) received a formal award from the Barcelona city council and so may be regarded as the official winner of the Modernista contest. However, of the three buildings in the group, it is the one to have suffered the most abuse. Decades ago the ground floor was gutted to make way for a shop, and valuable sculptures were carried off, including important works by Eusebi Arnau. To get an idea of how it might have looked, study the upper façade - a fantasy of ivory-coloured spires, complete with turret. Most of the sumptuous interior, including the wooden fixtures by Gaspar Homar, has also disappeared; the parts that do survive are hidden behind closed office doors. But you can see pictures of the original dining room, ethereally lit by the stained glass doors at the back, on most postcard stands in the city.

Antoni Tàpies Foundation

OPEN	Tues–Sun 10.00–20.00
CLOSED	Mon, except PH
CHARGES	€4.20; students and senior citizens €2.10; free for under 16s
TELEPHONE	**934 870 315**
WWW.	**fundaciotapies.org**
MAIN ENTRANCE	C/Aragó 255
DISABLED ACCESS	Yes
METRO	Passeig de Gràcia
SHOP	Excellent selection of books and prints relating to modern and contemporary art, architecture and photography; for works by Tàpies go to the **Galleria Toni Tàpies** at C/Consell de Cent 282, **T 834 876 402**

Around the corner from the Casa Lleó i Morera is another of Domènech i Montaner's designs, an early project (1881-6), built to house the Montaner i Simon publishing company. A recent addition, provocatively perched on top of the building, is a massive abstract sculpture, *Cloud with Chair*, which announces its present tenant, the foundation of contemporary Barcelona artist, Antoni Tàpies.

THE BUILDING

This was Domènech i Montaner's first commission in Barcelona, designed before his mature Modernista style had developed. With its red-brick construction and large glass surfaces, it brings to mind both Mudéjar and Gothic influences. As such it is more angular and geometric than most Modernista works, and lacks the organic motifs which came to characterize that style. While its exterior reflects the influence of traditional Catalan architecture, its wrought-iron decorated interior represents the optimism and pragmatism of the industrial age. Muntaner i Simon also employed Montaner to build his private home, the Casa Montaner, at C/Mallorca 278.

THE FOUNDATION

Antoni Tàpies was born (in 1923) into the Barcelona middle class milieu that was responsible for promoting Modernisme in the city. He first gained notoriety in 1948 as a co-founder of the Dau al Set group, and in 1950 was chosen to represent Spain at the Venice Biennale. From 1967 he began to experiment increasingly with different media, including clay and marble dust, producing the textured abstract works for which he is best known. In the early 1970s he participated in the pro-Democracy movement and produced important works of art theory. Today his foundation is home to a library and gallery which contains not only a comprehensive collection of his body of work, but also those of other international contemporary artists. The collection charts Tàpies career, from his Miró and Picasso-inspired early works through to his most recent donations, including *Home Anatòmic* (2002). The disquieting *Tres ulls* (*Three Eyes*, 2001) and *Matèria dels ulls* (*The Returning Gaze*, 2001) typify his fusion of sculpture and painting. Look out, too, for *Ocre i gris sobre marró* (1962) and the ceramic work, *Trespeus* (1985).

PEDRALBES AND BEYOND

At the same time that the grid of streets known as the Eixample was laid out in the mid-19c, a third Barcelona emerged along the periphery of the city. Here, just below the wooded hills of Collserola, the very wealthy built mansions and estates to supplement their townhouses. The epicentre of this development was the zone known as Pedralbes ('White Stones') which had been an area favoured by the medieval Catalan royalty. Pedralbes, along with Upper Gràcia and Horta to the east and the Zona Universitat to the west, contains a number of not-to-be-missed sites, including Park Güell and the Barcelona branch of the Thyssen Collection. Hilly, and not so easily reached by public transport, it takes more effort to explore these areas but is worth the exertion.

Park Güell

OPEN	Mon-Sun: May-Sept 10.00-20.00; Oct, March and April 10.00-19.00; Nov-Feb 10.00-18.00; 6/1 and 25-26/12 10.00-14.00
CLOSED	1/1
CHARGES	Free admission to park. Museum €3. Bus Turístic discount and free with Ruta del Modernisme voucher
TELEPHONE	Park **932 130 488**, Museum **932 193 811**
MAIN ENTRANCE	C/Olot
METRO/BUS STOP	Bus 24 from Passeig de Gràcia, or metro to Lesseps, then bus 24 or 15-minute uphill walk. Also on Bus Turístic route
SHOP	Good bookshop and gift shop with Gaudí-related souvenirs
EATING	There are indoor and outdoor cafés in the park

Arriving by bus you enter the park at the side entrance on Carretera del Carmel. To follow the route outlined below, walk through to the main gate at the bottom of the park on the C/Olot.

In the Park Güell Gaudí created the ultimate fusion between architecture and nature. The park was originally intended as a garden city on the lines of English models such as Bedford Park, the pioneering west London 'garden suburb', built by John Innes in the 1850s. Commissioned in 1900 by Eusebi Güell, the site was an estate of 15 hectares on the slopes of the unpromisingly named Mont Pelat or Bare Mountain, 150m above sea level overlooking the city. The desolate nature of the surroundings and

Park Güell

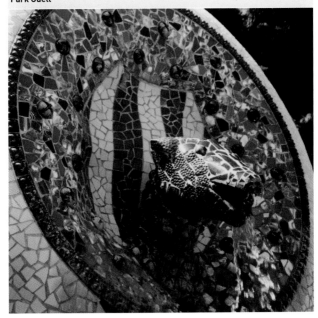

the traditional poverty of the neighbourhood partly explain why Güell's ambitious plans for the urban renewal of the area went awry. The project was ahead of its time and only two of the projected 60 houses were built. Gaudí moved into one of these himself, and the house is now a museum. He completed his work here in 1914, and in 1922 the city council acquired the abandoned garden city and opened it as a municipal park. The Park Güell, despite failing its original purpose, has proved to be the most loved of all Gaudí's works, and has provided inspiration to countless visitors, including the young Salvador Dalí, who considered the place as one of the most powerful influences on his development as an artist.

ENTRANCE The entrance is marked by two fantastically-shaped and richly-polychromed pavilions that look as if they are made of gingerbread. At the time the park was being designed, Gaudí was

Park Güell Pavilion roof

also contributing ideas to a production of Hänsel and Gretel at the Liceu theatre. It is therefore likely that his sketches – for the witch's and the children's houses - were transformed into the gatehouses. The one on the right as you face the park is topped by a fly agaric mushroom, created from broken red and white tiles. Gaudí was a keen mushroom-gatherer, and there has been much speculation as to why he chose this hallucinogenic variety to

Park Güell Ironwork gate

welcome people to the park. The left-hand gatehouse features a distinctly phallic mushroom, topped with a cross. This structure now houses a book and giftshop. The gate between the two pavilions is formed of spiky ironwork gates taken from Gaudí's Casa Vicens. The staircase immediately inside the park is elaborately decorated with ceramics and fountains, dominated by a glittering multicoloured lizard or dragon.

HALL OF THE 100 COLUMNS The steps lead up to the Sala Hipóstila, a large covered area intended to house the market serving the estate. The space, though known as the 'Hall of the 100 Columns', is in fact held up by 86 Doric columns. The ones at the front lean towards the centre, supporting an undulating entablature punctuated by dogs' heads. The intricate mosaic decoration was the work of Josep Maria Jujol, who was responsible for all the ceramic work in the park.

CERAMIC BENCH Above this is the famous bench-balustrade surrounding the park's central square, the **Plaça del Teatre Grec**. It is joined to the lower part of the park by flights of steps on either side of the Sala Hipóstila. The balustrade, which incorporates what is said to be the longest bench in the world, is a typical touch of Gaudí fantasy and symbolism. Shaped like a dragon, which serves to protect the estate, it glistens with a magnificent ceramic coating (*trencadís*) executed by Gaudí in collaboration with Jujol. There is a panoramic view of Barcelona from the square, and there are few better places from which to admire the city than the sinuous bench. On either side of the square are viaducts with leaning columns and an overall rustic appearance.

GAUDÍ MUSEUM The museum is housed in a building designed by Francesc Berenguer in 1904, which Gaudí acquired as a family home in 1906. The displays include furniture designed by Gaudí for other buildings, as well as his own wardrobe, iron bed and personal belongings.

Park Güell Ceramic bench (detail)

Park Güell Ceramic bench

Pedralbes Monastery

OPEN	10.00–14.00
CLOSED	Mon; 1/1, Good Friday, 1/5. 24/6, 25-26/12
CHARGES	€5.50, which includes admission to the **Thyssen-Bornemisza Collection**. €3.50, reduced admission for students under 25 years old, the unemployed and senior citizens; also for holders of the Barcelona Card and Bus Turístic. Free admission for under 16s and for all on the first Sun of each month
TELEPHONE	**932 039 282**
WWW.	**museuhistoria.ben.es/eng/centres/pedralbes**
MAIN ENTRANCE	Baixada del Monastir 9
DISABLED ACCESS	The museum has been partially adapted for disabled access
METRO	FGC Reina Elisenda, Bus Turístic
SHOP	Book and gift shop

Guided tours are available. Photography and filming are not allowed.

Barcelona's medieval nobility were traditionally drawn to the clean air and open spaces of Collserola, close to but above the crowded capital, so when Elisenda de Montcada, noblewoman and widowed queen of Jaume II of Aragon decided to found a convent for the Order of Poor Clares in 1326, Pedralbes was an obvious choice of location. Far from the city centre, it had the good fortune to escape the unrest of the 19c and 20c which destroyed so many of Barcelona's churches. As one of the finest examples of Catalan Gothic architecture it embodies the medieval qualities which inspired Modernists like Gaudí and Domènech i Montaner.

THE MONASTERY

Today you are free to stroll around the elegant cloisters and the rooms of the monastery, where you will find a collection of medieval art treasures. At the centre is the exquisitely carved marble *tomb of Elisenda* (1364), restored by the sculptor Frederic

Pedralbes Monastery Cloisters

Marès. Another highlight is the **Chapel of St Michael**, decorated with the finest surviving wall paintings of 14c Catalonia. The murals, redolent of the art of Trecento Italy, were painted by Ferrer Bassa between 1343 and 1346. The scenes in the upper register depict the Passion of Christ, while those in the lower level are from the Life of the Virgin.

THE THYSSEN-BORNEMISZA COLLECTION

A selection of works from the famous Thyssen-Bornemisza Collection are displayed here, although there is talk of moving them to the National Museum of Catalan Art (p 123). The main gallery for the collection is in Madrid. The paintings displayed here were chosen for their relevance to the history of the monastery and include Fra Angelico's beautiful *Madonna of Humility* (1433-5), as well as works by Veronese, Titian, Tintoretto, Canaletto, Guardi, Cranach, Rubens, Zurbarán and Velázquez.

COL.LEGI DE LES TERESIANES

OPEN	Not usually open to public, but call to check occasional weekend opening
TELEPHONE	**932 123 354**
MAIN ENTRANCE	C/Ganduxer 85-105, in the Sarrià district of town, off Via Augusta
METRO	FGC Bonanova

This convent school, designed by Gaudí, was built on a very tight budget in 1889-90. The austerity of the huge brick structure packs a powerful visual punch, with tall, narrow windows with louvred blinds, and characteristic pinnacles on the four corners.

Inside, there are supremely elegant corridors formed of seemingly endless rows of white parabolic arches. These create a mesmeric effect which must exert a soothing influence on the 1300 children who attend the school. Although it was built more than a century ago, the building is in pristine condition, with most of Gaudí's original door handles and window latches still in place.

Col.legi de les Teresianes Façade

Col.legi de les Teresianes Corridors with parabolic arches

There are no keyholes on the outside of the building, so if a door is locked someone has to let you in from inside. This is because St Teresa of Avila, to whom the school is devoted, believed that the key to the soul is inside the individual; that if someone is not mentally open to other people, to ideas or experiences, there is no point in anyone or anything trying to get in.

COLONIA GÜELL

OPEN	Usually visible from exterior only
TELEPHONE	**932 045 250**
MAIN ENTRANCE	Av. de Pedralbes 7-15
METRO	Maria Cristina

The entrance gate, lodge and stables are the finest surviving elements of the Güell Estate, situated in what is now the elegant residential district of Pedralbes.

Gaudí created these structures in 1884-7, at a time when he was heavily influenced by Islamic architecture. The fantastically turretted and irregularly-shaped pavilions combine elaborate brickwork with coloured ceramics, whitewashed walls and painted decoration. The stable block is now a centre of Gaudí studies known as the **Cátedra Gaudí**. The main gate features some of his most extraordinary ironwork, expressively twisted to form what is known as the *Drac de Pedralbes*, or Dragon of Pedralbes. The dragon is a reference to the myth of the Hesperides, on which the concept of the entire estate was based. The positions of the stars of the dragon constellation are traced across the top of the dragon's head and body.

Colonia Güell Entrance gate

Palau Reial de Pedralbes

OPEN	Tues-Sat 10.00-18.00, Sun and PH 10.00-15.00
	Gardens during daylight hours
CLOSED	Mon; 1/1, Good Friday, 1/5, 24/6, 25-26/12
CHARGES	€3.50 (includes admission to the **Decorative Arts** and **Ceramic**
	Museums, plus the **Textile Museum**); reduced admission €2
	Free admission to the gardens
TELEPHONE	**932 805 024** and **932 801 621**
WWW.	**museuartsdecoratives.bcn.es** and **museuceramica.bcn.es**
MAIN ENTRANCE	Av. Diagonal 686
DISABLED ACCESS	Yes
METRO	Palau Reial

A major building of Noucentista Barcelona, the royal palace of Pedralbes was designed by Eusebi Bona i Puig and Francesc de Paula Nebot i Torrens. It was financed by public subscription. With the proclamation of the Republic in 1931 it became city property and was converted into a museum the following year.

THE GARDENS AND THE GAUDÍ FOUNTAIN

Laid out by the landscape architect Nicolau Rubió i Tudurí in 1925, the palace's gardens include three illuminated fountains by Carles Buïgas i Sans and another by Gaudí. Gaudí's fountain was designed for the Güell estate, which was built on a part of the land later given to the Spanish royal family for the palace. It was only discovered in 1983 during a clean-up operation. As you approach the palace up the central path, you will find it a short distance down a path to the left, just before the pool in front of the palace.

THE CERAMICS MUSEUM

The collection focuses on Spanish ceramics from the 11c to the present day. The earliest pieces, from Islamic al-Andalus, can be seen as clear precursors of Valencian wares of the 14c and 15c. Spanish pottery came into its own in the 16c to 18c and fine pieces from around Spain, including Aragon, Catalonia and Castile, are on display here. In particular, there are exhibits from major centres of ceramic production, such as Manises, Paterna and Teruel. The modern and contemporary section includes works by Picasso and Miró, as well as Modernista and Noucentista pieces by the seminal ceramic designer Antoni Serra Fiter.

THE DECORATIVE ARTS MUSEUM

This eclectic collection has sections ranging from jewellery to horse-drawn carriages. The industrial design section offers a good introduction to the crafts for which the city has become so famous, and includes work by leading designers such as Mariscal and Oscar Tusquets.

on route

EIXAMPLE

Casa Calvet, C/Casp 48. The only recognition that Gaudí received from the city while he was alive was for this building. It is the most restrained of the three residences he created in the Eixample district. Built in 1898-9 as a store and home for a textile merchant and his family, the Calvets, it features a flat, rusticated façade in Montjuïc stone crowned by two undulating pediments, strongly influenced by Catalan Baroque. Different types of mushroom adorn the first-floor gallery - Mr Calvet was an enthusiastic mushroom gatherer.

The hall features ceramic decoration as well as a lift designed by Gaudí. The furniture that he created for the Calvet store and office was the first among his designs to reveal strong naturalistic inspiration. These pieces are now part of the 19c and 20c collections of the Museu Nacional d'Art de Catalunya (MNAC). The smart restaurant on the ground floor has retained the original layout. Try to see the rear façade, visible from the inner courtyard, which is much more distinctive than the main one. Only the restaurant may be visited, *T* 934 134 012, *M* Urquinaona

Casa Fuster, Passeig de Gràcia 132. Closed to the public. Located just above where Diagonal cut across Passeig de Gràcia, this mansion was built between 1908 and 1911 by Domènech i Montanter, assisted by his son Pere; it marked the transition from the city to the semi-rural suburbs. The elaborate windows and balconies are a trademark of the architect. *M* Diagonal

Casa Serra, Rambla de Catalunya 126, Av. Diagonal 395. Built as a private residence by Puig i Cadalfach in 1903, this massive palace, now a government building, is replete with medieval elements. The sculptures on the exterior are the work of Arnau and Jujols – Arnau made the saws as a play on the owner's name (*serra* means saw in Catalan). Closed to the public. *M* Diagonal, *FGC* Provença

Casa Terrades or '**de les Punxes**', Av. Diagonal 416-420, Bruc 141-143, and Rosselló 260-262. Just past the Palau Baró de Quadras, Puig i Cadalfuch indulged his passion for the medieval in this spired urban castle, whose form may have been inspired by an altarpiece by the 15c Barcelona painter Lluis Dalmau. It represents the height of the architect's 'pink period'. Apparently a single building, it actually consists of three apartments commissioned for the three Terrades sisters. Closed to the public. *M* Verdaguer

Egyptian Museum of Barcelona, Clos Archaeological Foundation, C/Valencia 284. Open Mon-Sat 10.00-20.00, Sun 10.00-14.00, *T* 934 880 188, www.fundclos.com. The Clos collection of archaeological finds gives an informative insight into the lives of the ancient Egyptians. Temporary exhibitions. Guided tours. Book and gift shop. *M* Passeig de Gràcia

Francisco Godia Foundation, C/València 284. Wed-Mon 10.00-20.00, closed Tues, *T* 932 723 180, www.fundacionfgodia.org. Important collection of paintings, sculpture and ceramics from the 12c to 21c. Temporary exhibitions. *M* Passeig de Gràcia

Palau Baró de Quadras, Av. Diagonal 373, Rosselló 279. Commissioned by the Baron of Quadras and built by Puig i Cadalfach between 1900 and 1903, this exquisite building has two contrasting façades which blend Gothic and Plateresque elements. The radiant interior incorporates classical Roman and Islamic motifs in the ceramic floor and wall decorations. The interior will be accessible when the Museu de Música reopens here. *M* Diagonal

Parc Joan Miró, between C/Vilamarí, Aragó, Diputació and Tarragona. Open during daylight hours. This park, also known as the Parc del Excorxador because it occupies the former site of the city's slaughterhouse (Excorxador means to flay), is set at the western edge of the Eixample, between Sants train station and the Plaça d'Espanya. Its centrepiece is the towering and phallic, ceramic-covered sculpture *Dona i ocell* (*Woman and Bird*), made in 1982 by Joan Miró and Gardy Artigas. *M* Espanya, Tarragona

Perfume Museum, Passeig de Gràcia 39. Mon-Fri 10.30-13.30, 16.30-20.00; Sat 11.00-14.00; closed Sun and PH, *T* 932 160 121, www.museudelperfum.com. Charts the development of perfume making. Exhibits include scent bottles from ancient Egypt to the present day, including Greek, Roman, Arabic and Oriental examples. *M* Passeig de Gràcia

PEDRALBES AND BEYOND

Barcelona Football Club Museum, F.C. Barcelona Stadium, Av. Arístides Maillol, entrance 7 or 9. Open 10.00-18.30, 10.00-14.00 Sun and PH. *T* 934 963 600, www.fcbarcelona.es. Situated in the grandstand, displays chart the history of the club from its origins in 1899 to the present day, and include trophies, photographs, programmes and posters by Joan Miró, Antoni Tàpies and other famous artists. The guided tour takes in the changing rooms, the tunnels and the pitch. Temporary exhibitions. Shop. Café. *M* Collblanc, Maria Cristina. Bus Turístic

Casa Bellesguard, C/Bellesguard 16-20, just below the Ronda de Dalt B20. The structure was built in 1900-2 as a private house over the scant remains of a summer residence built in 1408 for Martí I, the last of the Catalan kings. The palace was known as Bellesguard after the Catalan for 'beautiful view'. The medieval site inspired Gaudí to create a neo-Gothic castle-like structure, surmounted by a tall spire supporting a cross. The building, regarded by some as Gaudí's secular masterpiece, is also one of his least known works. The well-preserved interior, which is now divided into apartments, is not open to the public, but visitors may walk around the large garden, which provides an excellent

Casa Bellesguard

Casa Vicens Detail of tiling on the exterior

view of the building's exterior. It is also worth walking around the corner into Carrer Valeta d'Arquer to get another perspective. **M** Penitents then bus 60, or **FGC** Av. Tibidado then bus 123

Casa Vicens, C/Carolines 18-24. Gaudí's first major work, Casa Vicens is heavily influenced by Islamic architecture. It was built in 1883-8 for Manuel Vicens Montaner, who owned a tile factory. Gaudí was presumably briefed to make full use of his patron's ceramic supply, and indeed the building is lavishly coated in coloured tiles. Unlike his later works, characterized by curving lines and broken tiles, here he used geometric patterns in straight lines. The fantastical ironwork on the façade includes lizards, dragons, snakes and other creatures, all with individual faces. The intricate railings, a section of which has been incorporated into the main entrance gate of the Park Güell, are now believed to be the work of Francesc Berenguer. The interior is closed to the public. **M** Fontana, Lesseps (between Av. Pricep 'Asturies and C/Gran de Gràcia, just below Lesseps)

Laberint d'Horta, Passeig dels Castanyers. Open daily 10.00-dusk; €1.85, free Tues & Sun. Barcelona's oldest formal garden (constructed between 1793 and 1804). The park consists of three formal terraces, and a medieval tower presiding over a topiary maze. A great spot for peaceful relaxation and for children. **M** Mundet

Gate and railings of the Miralles Estate, Passeig de Manuel Girona 55-61. Near the Güell estate, Gaudí designed the gate and railing for the estate belonging to Hermenegild Miralles, a renowned publisher and printer. Built in 1901-2, the structure features Gaudí's characteristic wavy lines. There are two openings: larger leaf-shaped one was for carriages. The pedestrian entrance retains its original ironwork gate. The tiles above the doorways are shaped like a tortoise shell. Adjacent there is a sculpture of *Gaudí* by Quim Camps, which was placed here in 1999 following the restoration of the structure. **M** Maria Cristina

Casa Muley Afid, Passeig de la Bonanova 55. Closed to the public. This is a post-Modernista work (1911–4), belonging to the final phase of Puig i Cadalfach's 'white period'. Its plain exterior and 'Oriental' stylings relate to its first owner, a Moroccan sultan who was in exile in Barcelona. **FGC** Sarrià

Parc de l'Espanya Indùstrial, off Sants train station. Open during daylight hours; free. Built on the site of the former Montada Textile works, this urban park, distinguished by its curious, giant light-fixtures, features a variety of outdoor sculptures, fountains and an artificial lake. **M** Sants-Estació

commercial galleries

Gallery hours are usually Tues-Sat 10.00-14.00 and 17.00-20.30.

Carles Taché, C/Consell de Cent 290, **T** 934 878 836, www.carlestache.com. Renowned contemporary artists from different generations, including Sean Scully, Jannis Kounellis, Cornelia Parker and Tony Cragg. **M** Passeig de Gràcia

Estrany-de la Mota, Passatge Mercader 18, **T** 932 157 051, www.estranydelamota.com. Interesting space showing work by Spanish and international artists including Thomas Ruff, Jean Marc Bustamente, Natividad Bermejo and Ana Prada. **M** Diagonal

Eude, C/Consell de Cent 278, **T** 934 879 386. Opened in 1975, the gallery specializes in work on paper and photography by major figures including Hockney, Beuys and Delauney. **M** Passeig de Gràcia

Gothsland, C/Consell de Cent 331, **T** 934 881 922. 19c Modernista art, sculpture and furniture by renowned figures. **M** Passeig de Gràcia

H2O, C/Verdi 152, **T** 934 251 801, www.h2o.es. Located in a Modernista house, this lively gallery shows art, photography, design and architecture and is worth seeking out after visiting the Park Güell. **M** Lesseps

Joan Gaspar, Pl. Dr. Letamendi 1, **T** 933 230 748. Founded in 1909, the gallery has shown Picasso, Dalí, Miró, Tàpies and Clavé, but also deals with young artists. **M** Passeig de Gràcia

Joan Prats, Rambla de Catalunya 54, **T** 932 160 290, www.galeriajoanprats.com. One of the most prestigious galleries in Spain, artists include Ràfols Casamada, Perejaume, Evru and Hannah Collins. **M** Passeig de Gràcia

Joan Prats Artgràfic, C/Balmes 34, **T** 934 881 398. Photography and prints by renowned artists. **M** Universitat

Jordi Barnadas, C/Consell de Cent 347, **T** 932 156 365, www.barnadas.com. Graphic work and painting by new and established artists, including Martín Chirino and Perico Pastor. **M** Passeig de Gràcia

Kowasa, C/Mallorca 235, **T** 934 873 588, www.kowasa.com. Exhibitions of work by emerging and well-known photographers, located in an Art Nouveau building designed by Enric Sagnier. **M** Diagonal

Llucia Homs, C/Consell de Cent 315, **T** 934 677 162. Lively space specializing in young Spanish and international artists. **M** Passeig de Gràcia

Manuel Barbie, C/Consell de Cent 321, *T* 93 487 4453. Specialist in early 20c Catalan art. *M* Passeig de Gràcia

Maria Jose Castellví, C/Consell de Cent 278, *T* 932 160 482, www.galeriamariajosecastellvi.com. High quality work by emerging Spanish and international artists, as well as shows by figures of historical importance. *M* Passeig de Gràcia

Metropolitana, Rambla de Catalunya 50, 1st floor, *T* 934 874 042. Painting, sculpture, photography, installations and performance art by mainly Catalan artists. *M* Passeig de Gràcia or Catalunya

René Metras, C/Consell de Cent 331, *T* 934 875 874. The Metras family has been promoting avant-garde art for more than 40 years, showing major figures and young artists. *M* Passeig de Gràcia

Senda, C/Consell de Cent 337, *T* 934 876 759. Painting, sculpture, installations and photography by emerging and established artists. *M* Passeig de Gràcia

Senda-Espai 292, C/Consell de Cent 292, *T* 934 875 711. This space is used to show new work or to display the art of established artists in unusual ways. *M* Passeig de Gràcia

Toni Tàpies, C/Consell de Cent 282, *T* 934 876402 www.tonitapies.com. Original work and prints by major artists including Antoni Tàpies, Sol LeWitt, Antoni Llena and Jaume Plensa. *M* Passeig de Gràcia

3 Punts, C/Aribau 75, *T* 934 512 348. www.3punts.com. Concentrates on new work, with some exhibitions by established artists. Artists include José Hernández, Miquel Magem and Adrà Lanuza. *M* Passeig de Gràcia

eating and drinking

€ **El Japonés**, Passatge de la Concepció 2, *T* 934 872 592. Sushi and other Japanese delicacies in popular designer bar. Near La Pedrera. *M* Diagonal

Il Refugio, C/París 209, *T* 932 185 163. Family-run Italian place with homemade pasta and good risottos. *M* Diagonal

La Batequilla, C/Girona 88, *T* 9365660. Pretty vegetarian place with a very reasonable set-price lunch. *M* Girona

La Bodegueta, Rambla de Catalunya 100, *T* 932 154 894. Traditional tapas bar with marble tables and wine barrels. Good sandwiches. *M* Diagonal

La Muscleria, C/Mallorca 290, *T* 934 589 844. Boisterous Belgian restaurant specializing in mussels and French fries. *M* Diagonal

La Piazzenza, Av. Gaudí 27-29, *T* 934 363 817. Tasty homemade pizzas and tapas near Sagrada Família. Outdoor tables. *M* Sagrada Família

Laie Llibreria Café, C/Pau Claris 85, *T* 933 027 310. Comfortable café above a great bookshop. Serves good snacks and meals, with occasional live music, exhibitions and other events. *M* Passeig de Gràcia or Urquinaona

L'Hostal de Rita, C/Aragó 279, *T* 934 872 376 but no booking. Elegant colonial bistro décor. Excellent value fixed-price and à la carte menus make this a popular choice. Worth queuing. *M* Passeig de Gràcia

Mauri, Rambla de Catalunya 102, *T* 932 151 020. Huge range of fancy sandwiches, canapés and cakes. Also set lunch. *M* Diagonal

Mezzanine, C/Provença 236, *T* 934 548 798. Vegetarian food from around the world. Good wines and elegant décor. Near La Pedrera. *M* Diagonal

Non Solo Pizza, C/Enric Granados 110, *T* 932 181 920. Tasty, homemade Italian food; good desserts. *M* Diagonal

Pekín, C/Rosselló 202, *T* 932 150 177. Chinese restaurant that has won awards for its design. Menu combines Mandarin and Cantonese specialities, with plenty for vegetarians. Near La Pedrera. *M* Diagonal or *FGC* Provença

Río Azul, C/Balmes 92, *T* 932 159 333. First-class Cantonese cuisine in an elegant setting. Good selection of vegetarian dishes. Near Fundació Tàpies. *M* Passeig de Gràcia

€€ **Arrosseria Xàtiva**, C/Valencia 360, *T* 934 583 418. Busy Valencian restaurant for excellent paella and other rice dishes. Outdoor tables. *M* Verdaguer

Café d'Alep, C/Mallorca 308, *T* 934 591 607. Quirky café with Mediterranean food. Range of cavas and wines. Open until 2.30. *M* Verdaguer

De Tapa Madre, C/Mallorca 301, *T* 934 593 134. Good quality tapas in busy bar, which also has indoor and outdoor tables and is open from breakfast time. *M* Verdaguer

El Yantar de la Ribera, C/Roger de Flor 114, *T* 932 656 309. Excellent lamb and suckling pig, roasted in woodburning ovens. Specialities from the province of Burgos. Good wines and cigars. *M* Tetuán

Gargantúa y Pantagruel, C/Còrsega 200, *T* 934 532 020. Family-run, specializing in the cuisine of the Lleida province in Catalunya. Long list of Spanish and French wines. *M* Hospital Clínic

Hanoi, Plaça Doctor Letamendi 27, *T* 934 515 686. Authentic Vietnamese cuisine in elegant setting. Near the Tàpies Foundation. *M* Passeig de Gràcia

La Maison du Languedoc-Rouissillon, C/Pau Claris 77, *T* 933 010 498. Renowned French provincial cuisine with fantastic cheeses and patés. *M* Catalunya or Urquinaona

L'Encís, C/Provença 379, *T* 934 576 874. Sophisticated Catalan cuisine in intimate space near the Sagrada Família. Excellent quality food at reasonable prices. *M* Sagrada Família

Mantequería Ravell, C/Aragó 313, *T* 934 575 114. Delicatessen with a long shared table at the back. Great for a sandwich, drink or full meal. *M* Girona

Melton, C/Muntaner 189, *T* 933 632 776, www.restaurante-melton.com. Gourmet Italian cuisine in well-designed restaurant. Spanish and Italian wines, and range of grappas. *M* Hospital Clínic

Negro, Av. Diagonal 64, *T* 934 059 444. Lively, fashionable place with tasty international cuisine. Open until 2.00 at weekends. *M* María Cristina

Out of China, C/Muntaner 100, *T* 934 515 555. Elegant contemporary design and updated traditional food make this a very different Chinese restaurant. *M* Hospital Clínic

Semproniana, C/Rosselló 148, *T* 934 531 820. Quirky décor and creative Mediterranean cooking make this one of the most popular restaurants in the area. *M* Hospital Clínic or Diagonal

Thai Gardens, C/Diputació 273, *T* 934 879 898. Broad range of Thai dishes. The taster menu comprises 12 dishes and is good value. Ask for one of the traditional Thai tables. Near the Fundació Tàpies. *M* Passeig de Gràcia

Tragaluz, Passatge de la Concepció 5, *T* 934 870 196. Fashionable, romantic and stylish with lots of vegetarian and light dishes. Near La Pedrera. *M* Diagonal

Xix Kebab, C/Còrsega 193, *T* 933 218 210. Syrian restaurant with excellent mezze and exotic décor. *M* Hospital Clínic

€€€**Beltxenea**, C/Mallorca 275, *T* 932 153 024. Exquisite Basque cuisine with Catalan influences. Very smart in Modernista building with a lovely garden for eating outside in summer and first-class wine cellar. *M* Passeig de Gràcia

Casa Calvet, C/Casp 48, *T* 934 134 012. The combination of the setting - a Gaudí building decorated with tiling and stained glass - and chef Miguel Alija's Mediterranean cuisine make this one of the best restaurants in town. *M* Catalunya or Urquinaona

Casa Darío, C/Consell de Cent 256, *T* 934 533 135. Galician restaurant serving first-class seafood. Not cheap, but prices are fair given the quality. *M* Passeig de Gràcia or Universitat

Drolma, Hotel Majestic, Passeig de Gràcia 68, *T* 934 967 710. Extremely elegant gourmet restaurant with exquisite dishes created by Fermí Puig. *M* Passeig de Gràcia

El Raco d'en Freixa, C/Sant Elíes 22, *T* 932 097 559. One of the best restaurants in Spain. Innovative Catalan cuisine with excellent service. *FGC* Plaça Molina

Gorria, C/Diputació 421, *T* 932 451 164. Top-quality seasonal ingredients are used to prepare superb Basque cuisine. Near Sagrada Família. *M* Monumental

Hisop, Passatge Marimon 9, *T* 932 413 233. Highly creative Catalan cuisine in intimate setting. Taster menu. *M* Hospital Clínic or *FGC* Gràcia

Jean Luc Figueras, C/Santa Teresa 10, *T* 934 152 877. Innovative cuisine in elegant restaurant with only ten tables. Taster menu and excellent desserts. *M* Diagonal

La Dama, Avinguda Diagonal 423, *T* 932 020 686. Lavish dishes in sumptuous Modernista setting. *M* Diagonal

Ot, C/Torres 25, *T* 932 847 752. A real gourmet experience in a refreshingly informal restaurant. Chefs trained at El Bulli create a seven-course set menu. Only seven tables. *M* Diagonal

Roig Robi, C/Séneca 20, *T* 932 189 222. Sensational market cuisine by Mercé Navarro and her daughter Inma Crossas. Courtyard tables. **M** Diagonal

Saüc, Passatge Lluís Pellicer 12, **T** 933 210 189. Renowned chef Xavier Franco creates innovative versions of traditional Catalan dishes. Excellent value set lunch. **M** Hospital Clínic

BARS & CLUBS

Aire, C/Valéncia 236, **T** 934 515 812. Open 23.00-3.00. Popular women-only bar with dance floor and pool table. **M** Passeig de Gràcia

Dietrich, C/Consell de Cent 255, **T** 934 517 707. Open 22.00-3.00. Stylish gay club on two floors that gets very busy at weekends. Live performances. **M** Universitat

Domèstic, C/Diputació 215, **T** 934 531 661. Open 19.00-3.00. Bar with sofas where you can actually talk. Jazz, Latin and drum'n'bass music. Also restaurant. **M** Universitat

Dry Martini, C/Aribau 162-166. Open 18.30-3.00. Classic bar for serious cocktail connoisseurs. **M** Diagonal

Jazz Room at La Cova del Drac, C/Vallmajor 33, **T** 933 191 789, www.masimas.com. Open 23.00-5.00. Live jazz followed by dancing to jazz-house and Latin music. **FGC** Muntaner

La Boîte, Av. Diagonal 477, **T** 933 191 789. Live jazz in friendly club. **M** Hospital Clínic

Risco, C/Balmes 49, **T** 932 724 980, www.nightsungroup.com. Open 23.00-3.00. Bar with dancefloor that gets busy around midnight, much earlier than most clubs. **M** Passeig de Gràcia

Samba Brasil, C/Lepant 297, **T** 934 561 798. Open 18.30-3.00. Unpretentious Brazilian-run cocktail bar with good mix of people. **M** Sagrada Família

Santé Café, C/Comte d'Urgell 171, **T** 933 237 832. Open Mon-Fri 8.00-3.00, Sat-Sun 17.00-3.00. Fashionable café decorated in orange and white. Outdoor tables. DJs at the weekends. Good for a soothing breakfast on weekdays too. **M** Hospital Clínic

Smooth, C/Enric Granados 73, **T** 935 321 503. Open 20.00-3.00. Lounge bar specializing in wine, with wide range from mainly Spanish regions. Also restaurant. Occasional live music.**M** Diagonal or **FGC** Provença

Snooker, C/Roger de Llúria 42, **T** 933 179 760. Open 19.00-4.00.

Cocktail bar with velvet sofas and snooker and pool tables. Won a design award when it opened in 1985. Still popular. *M* Girona

Z:Eltas, C/Casanova 75, *T* 934 541 902. Open 22.30-3.00. Elegant gay bar with good-looking clientele. Woman friendly. Disabled access. *M* Urgell

shopping

ACCESSORIES

Loewe, Passeig de Gràcia 35, *T* 932 160 400. Exquisite clothes and accessories in leather and other fabrics, located in the Modernista Casa Lleó Morera. *M* Passeig de Gràcia

Mandarina Duck, Passeig de Gràcia 44 and C/Rosselló 218, *T* 934 883 226. Stylish bags and luggage in unusual colours and fabrics. *M* Passeig de Gràcia or Diagonal

Ramon Santaeularia, Rambla de Catalunya 40, *T* 934 878 720. Accessories, costume jewellery and huge range of buttons. *M* Passeig de Gràcia

ANTIQUES

Antic Interiors, C/Diputació 290, *T* 933 122 534. Wide selection of furniture and fabrics from many periods. *M* Passeig de Gràcia

Boulevard dels Antiquaries, Passeig de Gràcia 55, *T* 932 154 499. Gallery of dozens of antique shops with specialities including toys, ceramics and jewellery. *M* Passeig de Gràcia

Consejo de Arte, C/Consell de Cent 323, *T* 934 880 200. Art Nouveau and Art Deco furniture and objects. *M* Passeig de Gràcia

BOOKS

Altaïr, Gran Vía de les Corts Catalanes 616, *T* 933 427 171, www.altair.es. Specialist travel bookshop with wide selection of guidebooks and magazines. *M* Universitat

BCN Books, C/Roger de Llúria 118, *T* 933 763 343. English novels, guidebooks, dictionaries and cards. *M* Passeig de Gràcia

Casa del Llibre, Passeig de Gràcia 62, *T* 932 723 480, www.casadellibro.com. Wide selection of all sorts of books, including guidebooks and books in English. *M* Passeig de Gràcia

Crisol, C/Consell de Cent 341 and Rambla de Catalunya 81, *T* 932 152 720. Selection of English books, as well as magazines, videos and music. *M* Passeig de Gràcia

Laie, C/Pau Claris 85, *T* 933 181 739, www.laie.es. Good art, design and photography sections. Also stocks English books and has a great café upstairs. *M* Passeig de Gràcia or Urquinaona

CERAMICS

Lladró, Passeig de Gràcia 11, *T* 932 701 253, www.lladro.com. Flagship store of prestigious producer of porcelain figures. *M* Passeig de Gràcia

Sargadelos, C/Provença 274, *T* 932 150 368. Hand-painted work from the Royal Factory of Sargadelos in Galicia. *M* Diagonal

CIGARS

El Jardí de l'Havana, C/Pau Claris 145. Huge range of top-quality cigars. *M* Passeig de Gràcia

CLOTHES

Adolfo Domínguez, Passeig de Gràcia 32 and 89, *T* 934 874 170. One of Spain's most renowned designers, Domínguez designs elegant men's and women's clothes using beautiful fabrics. Also accessories and perfume. *M* Passeig de Gràcia

Antonio Miró, C/Consell de Cent 349-351, *T* 934 870 670, www.antoniomiro.es. Leading Catalan designer who makes understated yet unusual clothes for men and women. *M* Passeig de Gràcia

Antoni Pernas, C/Consell de Cent 314, *T* 934 871 667. Galician designer who produces elegant, contemporary clothes. *M* Passeig de Gràcia

Armand Basi, Passeig de Gràcia 49, *T* 932 151 421. Catalan label that produces funky day and clubwear. *M* Passeig de Gràcia

Bad Habits, C/València 261, *T* 934 872 259. Own collection of unusual pieces. *M* Passeig de Gràcia

Boulevard Rosa, Passeig de Gràcia 55. Shopping centre with more than a hundred boutiques stocking designer clothes, shoes and accessories. *M* Passeig de Gràcia

Camisería Pons, C/Gran de Gràcia 49, *T* 932 177 292. Beautiful shop in Modernista building. Designers include Amaya Arzuaga, Josep Abril and Lydia Delgado. *M* Fontana or *FGC* Gràcia

David Valls, C/València 235, *T* 934 871 285. Catalan designer who specializes in avant-garde knitwear for men and women. *M* Passeig de Gràcia

For Pilots, C/Mallorca 273, *T* 932 158 102. New and vintage leather flying jackets. *M* Diagonal

Harbort Leather Design, C/Martínez de la Rosa 54, *T* 932 185 890. Unique pieces by leather specialists. Made-to-measure service too. *M* Fontana, *FGC* Gràcia

Jean Pierre Bua, Av. Diagonal 469, *T* 934 397 100. One of the best boutiques in Barcelona. Stocks Dries van Noten, Gaultier, Alexander McQueen, Sybilla, Marni and other leading labels. *M* Diagonal

José Tomás, C/Mallorca 242, *T* 932 157 429. Leading menswear designer renowned for giving classical cuts a quirky twist. *M* Diagonal

Josep Font, C/Provença 304, *T* 934 872 110, www.josepfont.com. One of Catalunya's top young designers, who makes beautifully crafted clothes with exquisite details. *M* Diagonal

Lydia Delgado, C/Minerva 21, *T* 934 159 998. One of Barcelona's top designers, who creates feminine clothes in soft fabrics. *M* Diagonal

Mango, Passeig de Gràcia 8-10 and 65, *T* 934 121 599. The latest styles at budget prices. Also stocks bags and shoes. *M* Passeig de Gràcia

Menkes, Gran Vía de les Corts Catalanes 646, *T* 933 188 647. Embroidered shawls, flamenco dresses and shoes.

    M Passeig de Gràcia

Miró Jeans, C/València 272, *T* 932 722 491. Antonio Miró's younger line, designed by José Castro. *M* Passeig de Gràcia

M69, C/Muntaner 69, *T* 934 536 259. Menswear by Helmut Lang, Paul Smith and Dirk Bikkembergs. Also books and music. *M* Universitat

Puravida, Plaça Rius i Taulet 11, *T* 932 386 722. Seek out this shop in the Gràcia area for one-off pieces by Argentinian designers. *FGC* Gràcia

Purificación García, Passeig de Gràcia 21, *T* 934 877 292. Elegant designs in beautiful fabrics and muted tones. *M* Passeig de Gràcia

Roberto Verino, Passeig de Gràcia 68, *T* 934 672 015. Renowned designer from Galicia. Men's and women's collections. *M* Passeig de Gràcia

Zara, Rambla de Catalunya 67, C/València 245 and other branches, *T* 934 877 0818. Excellent low-price chain for men, women and children. *M* Passeig de Gràcia

Zas, C/Mallorca 275, *T* 932 151 603. Men's and women's clothes by Custo, David Valls, Armand Basi and other leading designers. *M* Diagonal

Zona Eleven, C/Muntaner 61 and C/Diputació 188, *T* 934 537 145. Menswear by Roberto Cavalli, Versace, Dolce & Gabbana and Frederic Homs. *M* Universitat

FOOD

Cacao Sampaka, C/Consell de Cent 292, *T* 932 720 833. Top-quality chocolate with some highly unusual fillings, including olives, curry and blue cheese, all in beautiful minimalist packaging. Café at the back. *M* Passeig de Gràcia

Colmado Quílez, Rambla de Catalunya 63, *T* 932 152 356. Delicatessen renowned for its superb range of groceries. *M* Passeig de Gràcia

Queviures Murria, C/Roger de Llúria 85, *T* 932 155 789. Delicatessen in a Modernista building which stocks a wide selection of Catalan and Spanish foods and wines. *M* Passeig de Gràcia

HOBBIES

Dona, C/Provença 256, *T* 934 882 784. Everything for needlework enthusiasts. *M* Diagonal

Puzzlemanía, C/Diputació 225, *T* 934 515 803. Enormous selection of jigsaws and other games. *M* Catalunya

HOME & DESIGN

BD Ediciones, C/Mallorca 291, *T* 934 586 909, www.bdbarcelona.com. Essential stop for anyone interested in Barcelona's design heritage, with reproductions of Gaudí pieces and work by leading contemporary designers, displayed in Modernista building. *M* Passeig de Gràcia

Dom, Passeig de Gràcia 76, *T* 934 871 181. Quirky contemporary lamps and objects for the home. *M* Passeig de Gràcia

El Taller de Lencería, C/Rosselló 273. Beautiful bedding. Embroidered tablecloths and sheets. *M* Diagonal

Imagine, C/Enric Granados 67, *T* 934 530 171. Furniture by designers including Oscar Tusquets, Jorge Pensi and Edaurd Samsó. *M* Passeig de Gràcia

Pilma, Av. Diagonal 403, *T* 934 161 399, www.pilma.com. Design emporium with enormous selection of kitchen and bathroom equipment, as well as furniture and lighting. *M* Diagonal

Punto Luz, C/Pau Claris 146, *T* 932 160 393. Lamps by leading and emerging designers. *M* Passeig de Gràcia

Vinçon, Passeig de Gràcia 96, *T* 932 156 050. Barcelona's principal temple to modern design, with a vast range of household goods, furniture and accessories, all presented in witty, original guises. Temporary exhibitions. *M* Diagaonal

JEWELLERY

Aureli Bisbe, C/Pau Claris 178, *T* 932 154 841. Renowned designer who has created jewellery inspired by Barcelona monuments. *M* Diagonal

Bagués, Passeig de Gràcia 41, *T* 932 160 174. Housed in the Casa Amatller, prestigious jeweller stocks Modernista jewellery by Masriera i Carreras. *M* Passeig de Gràcia

Joaquín Berao, C/Rosselló 275, *T* 93 217 7032. One of Spain's top contemporary jewellery designers. *M* Diagonal

Maurer, Rambla de Catalunya 52, *T* 932 160 227. Wide range of well-known brands of watches. *M* Passeig de Gràcia

Roca, Passeig de Gràcia 18, *T* 933 183 266. Beautiful shop designed by Josep Lluís Sert, in business since 1888. Traditional and contemporary designs. *M* Passeig de Gràcia

Tous, Passeig de Gràcia 75, *T* 934 881 558. Unusual contemporary and traditional jewellery. *M* Passeig de Gràcia or Diagonal

KIDS

Bóboli, C/Gran de Gràcia 98, *T* 932 375 670. Fun fashion for children of all ages. *M* Fontana

Mullor, Rambla de Catalunya 102, *T* 932 151 202. Funky clothes for babies and small children. *M* Diagonal

Tic-Tac, Av. Diagonal 550, *T* 932 006 313. Vast range of toys and sportswear. *M* Diagonal

LINGERIE

Janina, Rambla de Catalunya 94, *T* 932 150 484. High quality underwear, hosiery and toiletries. *M* Diagonal

La Perla, Rambla de Catalunya 88, *T* 934 677 149. Luxurious Italian underwear, swimwear and accessories. *M* Diagonal

La Perla Gris, C/Rosselló 220, *T* 932 152 991. Swimwear and lingerie by top labels. *M* Diagonal

MUSIC

FNAC, El Triangle shopping centre, Plaça Catalunya 4, *T* 933 441 800, www.fnac.es. All sorts of music, as well as books and electrical equipment. *M* Catalunya

Planet Music, C/Mallorca 214, *T* 934 514 288. Huge shop with pop, soul, jazz, flamenco and World music sections. *M* Diagonal

PHOTOGRAPHY

Lázaro, Passeig de Gràcia 58, *T* 932 157 666. Wide range of film and camera equipment. *M* Passeig de Gràcia

SHOES

Camper, C/València 249 and Rambla de Catalunya 122, *T* 932 156 390. Quirky shoes for men and women by renowned Mallorcan firm. *M* Passeig de Gracia, Diagonal

Carmina Albaladejo, Rambla de Catalunya 29, *T* 933 021 934. Handmade shoes from Mallorca in the softest leather. *M* Catalunya

Farrutx, C/Rosselló 218 and C/Diputació 255, *T* 932 150 685. Up-to-the-minute designs by top Balearic firm. *M* Diagonal

Jaime Mascaró, C/Muntaner 239, *T* 932 000 137. This designer uses the softest leather and suede to make his shoes and accessories. *M* Hospital Clínic

Jorge Juan, Rambla Catalunya 125 and C/Valencia 241, *T* 932 170 840. Exclusive shoes and bags. *M* Diagonal, Passeig de Gràcia

Le Shoe, C/Tenor Viñas 6, *T* 932 411 012. Shoes and bags by top international designers, including Marc Jacobs, Blumarine and Sonia Rykiel. *FGC* Muntaner

Lurueña, Av. Diagonal 580, *T* 932 096 889. Specialist in classic, elegant shoes. *M* Hospital Clínic

Muxart, C/Rosselló 230 and Rambla de Catalunya 47, *T* 934 881 064, www.muxart.com. Unique avant-garde shoes and accessories by leading Catalan designer. *M* Diagonal, Passeig de Gràcia

Tascón, Rambla de Catalunya 42 and Passeig de Gràcia 64, *T* 934 879 084. Fashionable shoes and boots for men and women by Catalan and international designers. *M* Passeig de Gràcia

Vogue, Passeig de Gràcia 30 and Rambla de Catalunya 33, *T* 933 019 035. Fashionable, good-quality shoes and bags. *M* Passeig de Gràcia

Yanko, Passeig de Gràcia 95, *T* 934 880 688. Top quality elegant shoes and bags. *M* Passeig de Gràcia

STATIONERY

Cent Detalls en Paper, C/Consell de Cent 332, *T* 934 880 490. Handmade paper with unusual designs. *M* Passeig de Gràcia

Konema, C/Consell de Cent 296, *T* 934 883 325. Beautiful stationery, pens, accessories and all sorts of gifts. *M* Passeig de Gràcia

Mon Ecològic, C/Mallorca 198, *T* 934 543 765. Paper, files and other items made from recycled materials. *M* Diagonal

WINE

Cata 181, C/València 181, *T* 933 236 818. Wide selection of still and sparkling wines. Also bar with interesting tapas. *M* Passeig de Gràcia

Lavinia, Av. Diagonal 605, *T* 933 634 445. Vast store with huge range of wines and expert staff. Tastings, courses and lectures. *M* Maria Cristina

La Carta de Vinos, C/Pau Claris 169, *T* 934 677 023. Huge selection of wines from around the world. *M* Passeig de Gràcia

Xampany, C/València 200, *T* 934 539 338. Specializes in cava, but also stocks good range of still wines. *M* Passeig de Gràcia

PICASSO MUSEUM
AND THE RIBERA

Until the grand avenues of the Eixample were laid out, the élite of Barcelona lived in fortress-like palaces that hemmed in the narrow lanes of the neighbourhood around the Church of Santa Maria del Mar. This neighbourhood, known as the Born, is part of the larger area called La Ribera which had been enclosed by city walls in the 1300s and originally included the site that is now Parc de la Ciutadella. In the 1800s, with the departure of the wealthy, this area declined, becoming a near slum by the mid-20c. But it was revitalized during the preparations for the 1992 Olympics and is now a centre of art, nightlife and fine dining, with the Picasso Museum bringing droves of visitors to its once quiet streets.

Picasso Museum

OPEN	Tues-Sat 10.00-20.00, Sun 10.00-15.00
CLOSED	Mon; 1/1, 1/5, 25-26/12
CHARGES	Permanent collection: €5; €2.50 reduced admission Temporary exhibitions: €5; €2.50 reduced admission Reduced admission for students under 25, senior citizens and the unemployed. Discount with Barcelona Card. Free for under 16s Free access for all first Sunday of each month
TELEPHONE	**933 196 310**
WWW.	**museupicasso.bcn.es**
MAIN ENTRANCE	C/Montcada 15-23
DISABLED ACCESS	There is good access for visitors with disabilities and wheelchairs are available
METRO	Jaume I
SHOP	Large shop with wide range of books on Picasso, other artists and Barcelona, plus cards, posters, prints, T-shirts, accessories and gifts
EATING	Café serving salads and sandwiches

*Temporary exhibitions concentrate on specific aspects of Picasso's work,
featuring material from the museum's extensive collections that is not included
in the permanent displays. The library may be visited by prior arrangement only.*

The museum opened in 1963, instigated by Jaume Sabartés,
Picasso's life-long friend and secretary. Picasso presented 58
works to the museum in 1968, including a famous series of
paintings and oil sketches relating to Velázquez's *Las Meninas*.
Then in 1970 he donated an enormous group of works that had
been executed in his youth, which had been kept over the years in
his sister's flat on the Passeig de Gràcia. After the artist's death
in 1973, his heirs, carrying out the conditions of his will, gave a
large body of his graphic work to the museum. In 1981, a
collection of 141 ceramics owned by his widow Jacqueline was
also donated.

THE BUILDING

The museum enjoys an exceptionally beautiful setting in five adjoining medieval mansions. The first is the Palau Berenguer d'Aguilar, which dates back to the 12c but was remodelled in the 15c-18c. From 1970 to 1981, the museum was gradually expanded into the Casa del Baró de Castellet, an 18c building with 15c fragments, and the Palau Meca, an 18c remodelling of a 14c structure. In 1999, it was substantially enlarged with a new series of rooms in the next two mansions, the 18c Casa Mauri and the Palau Finestres, parts of which date back to the 13c. In 2003, more rooms in these buildings were opened up, enabling the displays to be extended again.

HIGHLIGHTS

Portrait of Aunt Pepa	Room 7
Science and Charity	Room 8
The Embrace	Room 10
The Woman with the Cap	Room 11
Harlequin	Room 12
Las Meninas suite	Rooms 15-16
The Pigeons	Room 17

The museum has an unrivalled collection of the artist's early works. Academic drawings made as a child in Malaga and La Coruña (Rooms 2-3) put to the test the artist's later boast that he could draw like Raphael at the age of ten. Experiments with Impressionism, Pointillism and Symbolism gave way after 1901 to the development of a more personal style in the Blue Period and then the Pink Period, which are excellently represented in the museum (Rooms 11-14). These periods drew inspiration from scenes of poverty and hardship, observed in the streets of both Paris and Barcelona. The museum's holdings of later stages in Picasso's art are far from representative.

Picasso and Barcelona

Pablo Picasso (1881-1973), the most influential artist of the 20c, had a personal attachment to Barcelona. He was born in Málaga and raised in La Coruña, but his family moved to Barcelona in 1895 when he was 14 and had already had his first exhibition. Two years later, his talent established, Pablo moved to Madrid. In 1899 he returned to Barcelona and became involved with a group of avant-garde artists who were championing the Modernista movement, and who formed the core of the group which met regularly at the bar Els Quatre Gats (p 84). Picasso held his first Barcelona exhibition here in 1900, before departing for Paris. For the following four years, coinciding with his Blue Period, he moved back and forth between the two cities, and many of his works take as subjects the marginal characters of the decadent Barri Gòtic (Old City). It was in Paris in 1907 that he painted one of his first Cubist works, *Les Demoiselles d'Avignon* (MoMA, New York), the 'ladies' being prostitutes in a brothel of Barcelona's Avignon Street (C/Avinyó). Back in Barcelona in 1917 he painted the *Harlequin*, which can now be seen in the Picasso Museum. For most of the rest of his career he was based in the south of France, but the people of the Barri Gòtic continued to have an impact on his art throughout the rest of his rich and varied career.

FIRST FLOOR

The permanent collection is housed on the first floor. Turn right at the top of the staircase from the courtyard.

EARLY WORKS *Rooms 1-3* Picasso's earliest works are displayed in these three rooms. Born in Malaga in 1881, he moved with his family to La Coruña in Galicia in 1891, where his father taught at the art school. The expressive *Portrait of a Man with a Beret* in Room 2 was painted when he was 14 years old. A display case contains drawings including *The Lottery Seller* and *Lola Seated with a Doll*.

In 1895 his father was appointed Professor of Fine Arts at the Academy of Art in Barcelona (La Llotja), and the family moved here in September of that year. Picasso enrolled at La Llotja as a pupil. In Room 3 there is a self-portrait, a watercolour of his father and a pastel portrait of his mother.

1895-1901 *Rooms 4-10* On the other side of the central corridor, this section takes us from 1895 to 1901, during which period Picasso spent time in Malaga, Madrid, the village of L'Horta de Sant Joan, Barcelona and Paris.

Room 4 contains some small oil paintings on wood made in Barcelona in 1896, including *Coming Out of the Theatre*. From the same year are the seascapes in Room 6, which include *The Beach at La Barceloneta*, showing the chimneys of the textile mills of the Poble Nou district in the background.

In Room 7, *Portrait of Aunt Pepa*, painted in Malaga in 1896, shows how his brushwork and use of light were developing. The Picassos spent their summers at the family home in Màlaga. In 1896, Pablo's uncle Salvador asked the young man to paint his sister, Josefa Ruíz Blasco, 'Aunt Pepa'. The result is a haunting psychological portrait in which the stark will of the old woman is reflected in her piercing eyes and palely radiant face, set against a dark background.

Science and Charity, in Room 8, was his first large-scale work, painted to show at the National Fine Arts Exhibition in Madrid in 1897-8. It was this painting which first brought Picasso to the attention of the Madrid art establishment and earned him a prize at the city's annual Fine Arts and Design fair. The large canvas reflects a fin-de-siècle optimism in science as a vehicle for human progress and shows a doctor, modelled by Picasso's father, attending a sick woman. Also in this room is a series of paintings produced during his stay in the village of L'Horta de San Joan in 1898-9, which show a shift away from academic strictures to a more naturalistic style. When he returned to Barcelona he became a regular at Els Quatre Gats café, and the works displayed in Room 9 feature some of his friends from this period, as well as a portrait of his sister Lola. A change in the artist's style

MUSEU PICASSO
First Floor

A Sabartés Room
B Neoclassical Room
C Palaus Room

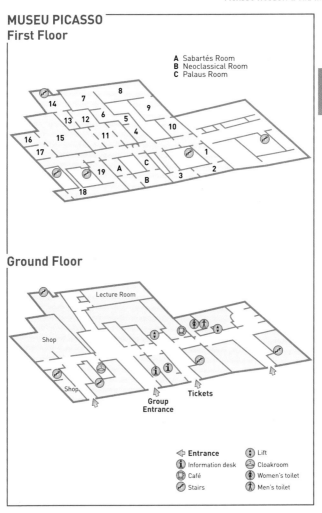

Ground Floor

Lecture Room

Shop

Shop

Tickets

Group
Entrance

◁ **Entrance**
ⓘ Information desk
🅒 Café
✦ Stairs

🛗 Lift
🅒 Cloakroom
🚺 Women's toilet
🚹 Men's toilet

is seen in *Carrer de la Riera de Sant Joan*, a view down to the busy, narrow street from the window of his studio, where the undefined shapes show how the artist was moving towards abstraction.

Picasso made his first visit to Paris in 1900, where he stayed in Montmartre. Room 10 displays work from this period, including *The Embrace* (1900) and *Margot* or *The Wait* (1901). Taking cues from Rodin, Toulouse-Lautrec, and Edvard Munch, the former is a simple but powerful image of two figures embracing, the colours blending their kiss into an undifferentiated form. In *Margot* or *The Wait*, one of the many portraits that Picasso painted on his arrival in Paris, the influence of Toulouse-Lautrec is still apparent, but now the artist breathes life into the figure through his exuberant use of colour.

Before visiting the rest of the collection, there is a room on the left off the central corridor which provides information about the buildings housing the museum. This leads into the **Neoclassical Room**, decorated in green and gold with a marble patterned floor, which is part of the Baro de Castellet mansion.

You return to the main corridor via a room devoted to **Jaume Sabartés**, whom Picasso met in 1899, when they were both 18 years old. Sabartés became Picasso's secretary as well as a close friend and was the catalyst behind the founding of this museum.

1901-1917 *Rooms 11-14* This section charts Picasso's development from 1901 to 1917, which encompasses his **Blue** and **Pink Periods** and his move into **Cubist** and **abstract forms**.

Picasso's Blue Period began in Paris in 1901, when he took over the studio of his friend Carles Casagemas, who had committed suicide a few months earlier. The paintings from this time are imbued with melancholy and suffering. The central part of Room 11 contains paintings of the rooftops of Barcelona, painted in 1902 when he was back in Barcelona and renting a studio on Carrer Nou de la Rambla, on the edge of the red-light district. In the right-hand side of the room is *The Woman with the Cap*, which was painted in Paris in 1901 and depicts an inmate at the women's prison of Sainte-Lazare. The *Woman with the Lock of Hair* and *The*

Forsaken were both painted in 1903 in Barcelona. In the left-hand section is the 1903 *Portrait of Sebastia Junyent*, his close friend, and also *Portrait of Mrs Canals*, painted in 1905 in Paris, which marks the beginning of his Pink Period.

In Room 12, *The Offering* (1908) displays another stylistic departure, with the introduction of Cubist elements. Also on display in this room is *Harlequin* (1917), perhaps the best-known work in the collection, which represents a return to Expressionism for Picasso. The subject of the painting is the choreographer of Diaghilev's famous Ballets Russes, Léonide Massine, whom Jean Cocteau had encouraged the artist to work with, and among whose dancers was Olga Kokhlova, who was to become Picasso's first wife.

The first abstract works are in Room 13, and include *Blanquita Suarez*, who sang and danced at the Teatre Tivoli in Barcelona. *Figure with Fruit Bowl* combines naturalism with Cubism.

In Room 14, *Passeig de Colom* shows the statue of Columbus from the window of the pension where he stayed in 1917. The charcoal drawing *Gored Horse* reflects Picasso's keen interest in bullfighting and heralds the expressionistic figures he would later create in his masterpiece *Guernica*.

THE 1950S *Rooms 15-17* At the end of the main corridor on the right, the exhibits in these three rooms jump forward 40 years to 1957, when Picasso painted a group of works inspired by Velázquez's *Las Meninas* (1656), which depicts Princess Margarita María and her ladies-in-waiting. Velázquez had transformed Picasso's vision when the artist, an adolescent in Madrid, discovered him in the collection of the Prado. Picasso's *Las Meninas* series comprises 85 studies in oil. Strongly Cubist, they represent an exhaustive creative probe into the very nature of painting and art. In the largest of these works Picasso recreates Velázquez's figures using only grey tones and substantially increasing the size of the figure of the artist himself. Room 16 displays small portraits of figures from the original painting.

Room 17 contains a group of works painted in Cannes in 1957, called *The Pigeons*, which were a theme of his work throughout his life.

LATER YEARS *Rooms 18-19* Cross the corridor again to the final two rooms, which deal with Picasso's late years. On display are a selection of his ceramics, including plates and jars decorated with animals and fish. Paintings include the self-portrait *Painter at Work* (1965), and *Seated Man* (1969).

Parc de la Ciutadella

OPEN	During daylight hours
ENTRANCE	From Pg/Picasso, Pg/Pujades and C/Wellington
METRO	Arc de Triomf

In 1715, as punishment for the city's resistance to the Bourbon faction in the Spanish War of Succession, the victorious Philip V ordered the burning of an entire section of La Ribera. On its site he built a powerful fortress, which along with the castle of Montjuïc could threaten the rebellious city with bombardment should it waver in its loyalty to the crown. The brooding fortress remained until 1859, when as part of the city's modernization it was demolished and covered over with a public park. The park is home to the Catalan Parliament and to the city's zoo. In 1888 it was the showcase for the Universal Exhibition, and a number of Modernista and Noucentista buildings were raised in the park and its environs, especially along the wide avenue now called the Passeig Lluís de Companys, which led up towards the northern train station.

THE PARK

The park itself is a semi-formal garden with broad grassy lawns hedged by trees gathered from around the world. It was laid out by the French landscape architect Jean-Claude Nicolas Forestier, and its focal point is a small parade ground, framed on one side by a small lake, the domain of rowing boats and swans, a bandstand, and a monumental fountain. The *Cascada* is a sculptural extravaganza of 1875-81 by Josep Fontseré which features the work of leading Catalan sculptors of the day, and was a key point of reference for the young Gaudí, who probably assisted in its construction. The rest of the park is dominated by the Catalan Parliament buildings, the city zoo (which may move to another site) and the **Museu d'Art Modern** (whose collection is being transferred to the National Museum of Catalan Art (MNAC) in 2004 (p 137). Overlooking Passeig de Picasso, the two glasshouses (the Umbracle of 1883-4 and the Hivernacle of 1884-8) and the Castle of the Three Dragons, which houses the zoological museum, were constructed in the 1880s. The site is also home to many works of 19c and 20c sculpture, the most notable of which is Tàpies' *Homage to Picasso*, located outside the park wall along Passeig de Picasso and installed in 1983.

Parc de la Ciutadella

Museu d'Art Modern

The collection at the Museu d'Art Modern is due to move to the Museu Nacional d'Art de Catalunya (MNAC) in June 2004. While it remains at is location in Parc de la Ciutadella, the opening times are Tues-Sat 10.00-19.00 and Sun 10.00-14.30.

THE BUILDINGS OF THE EXHIBITION OF 1888

The area around the Ciutadella was transformed for the 1888 Exhibition. Domènech i Montaner was contracted to design two new buildings: the Gran Hotel International (demolished after the

Arc de Triomf

exhibition) and a café-restaurant, now known as the Castell dels Tres Dracs. This work, with its undecorated brickwork and laminated steel framework, combined modern building techniques with the look of an elaborate medieval castle. After the exhibition ended it became the architect's studio and workshop and served as a prototype for many of his later projects. The plain brick walls feature decorative touches including heraldic symbols and paintings, wrought-iron work and a magnificent glazed turret.

The broad avenue leading up to Josep Vilaseca i Casanoves' red-brick **Arc de Triomf**, built as the entrance to the Universal Exhibition, was once flanked to the south by a monumental palace of the arts (destroyed by fascist bombs in the Civil War), and is now dominated by the main court house, the Palau de la Justicia (1887-1908), which marks a transitional style between Modernisme and Noucentisme.

Palau de la Música Catalana

OPEN	Mon-Sat 10.00-15.00, guided tours only (every half hour, lasting approximately 50 mins)
CHARGES	€7; students, senior citizens and unemployed, €6.50
TELEPHONE	**932 957 200**
WWW.	**palaumusica.org**
MAIN ENTRANCE	C/Sant Francesc de Paula 2
METRO	Urquinaona

This extraordinary Modernista masterpiece, declared a World Heritage Site by UNESCO in 1997, was commissioned from Lluís Domènech i Montaner in 1905 by the city's choral society, the

Palau de la Música Catalana

Orfeò Català. Faced with the challenge of building a full-sized concert hall in a restricted space, he devised a plan that placed the actual concert hall - a gigantic, glittering music box - on the second floor. Three years later, the building was inaugurated with a Richard Strauss concert performed by the Berlin Philharmonic.

Inside and out, the decoration of the Palau is overwhelmingly rich, ranging from monumental allegorical sculpture to dazzling ceramic mosaic and stained-glass. The *pièce de resistance* is the inverted glass cupola by Antoni Rigalt in the main concert hall, which seems to defy gravity – in fact, contemporaries who saw the plans declared it technically impossible. The stage itself is framed by magnificently kinetic sculpted horses by Pau Gargallo and an array of stone muses by Eusebi Arnau. The exterior sculpture is the work of Miquel Blay, and the striking mosaic which dominates the ground floor exterior is by Lluís Bru. The building's fixtures are all dominated by the characteristic Modernista obsession with decorative detail.

The Palau is the venue for regular series of concerts and events, which range from classical music to rock.

The Cathedral

OPEN	Mon-Fri 8.00-13.30, 16.00-19.30; Sat & Sun 8.00-13.30, 17.00-19.30. Museum daily 10.00-13.00, 17.00-19.00
CHARGES	Museum €1, choir €1, lift to roof €1.10
TELEPHONE	933 102 580
WWW.	bcn.es
MAIN ENTRANCE	Plaça de la Seu
DISABLED ACCESS	Good facilities
METRO	Jaume I
SHOP	Small range of religious objects, books and souvenirs

HIGHLIGHTS

4c Tomb of Santa Eulàlia

14c cloister

15c chapter house

Chapel of Christ of Lepanto

The openwork spires of the Cathedral dominate the Barri Gòtic, pushing their way high above the narrow surrounding streets and alleys. Its origins go back to an early Christian basilica of the 4c or 5c, the foundations of which can be seen in the basement of the Museu d'Història de la Ciutat. Destroyed by the Moorish leader Al-Mansur in 985, this was replaced in the mid-11c by a Romanesque structure.

The present Cathedral was begun in 1298, during the bishopric of Bernat Pelegri and the reign of Jaume II. The unknown first architect was succeeded in 1317 by the Mallorcan Jaume Fabre, who remained in charge of the works until his death in 1339, bringing to completion the apse, ambulatory and crossing. From 1358-88 the construction of the building was taken over by Bernat Roca or Roquer, who laid out most of the nave and initiated the construction of the cloister. Arnau Bargues, who was director of works after 1397, planned the magnificent chapter house, which was built in 1405-15. The choir, in the middle of the nave, was completed c 1460, after which the fabric of the Cathedral was little altered until the 19c.

EXTERIOR Work on the Cathedral was begun, unusually, at the south transept and the oldest feature of the exterior is the **Romanesque portal** overlooking the Plaça de Sant Iu. The portal, carved in marble and Montjuïc stone, is flanked by panels with inscriptions recording the commencement of work in 1298. Above these are carvings of a man with a griffin and a man battling with a lion, while in the tympanum itself is a figure believed to be Sant Iu (Ivo).

Among the most striking exterior architectural features are the two **octagonal towers** - dating from the 1380s - that rise above the

The Cathedral

transepts. The finest statuary is the late-15c wooden relief contained within the tympanum of the **Portal del Pietat**, which leads into the cloister. The late-19c west façade, with its three openwork spires and intricate decoration, was built by Josep Oriol Mestres and owes more to northern European architecture than to Catalan Gothic.

INTERIOR The three-aisled interior, with its blind triforium and tiny rose windows in the clerestory, is spacious and atmospheric. Large bosses decorate the Gothic cross-vaults, while a colonnade of tall piers forms a particularly elegant ambulatory. By far the most impressive of the chapels is the one dedicated to the **Christ of Lepanto** (to the right of the main entrance). Covered with an elaborate star-shaped vault richly adorned with bosses, this was originally the chapter house built in 1407 by Arnau Bargues. Its carved image of the *Crucifixion* is said to have been carried by Don John of Austria in the Battle of Lepanto (1571), where it was placed on the prow of his flagship *La Real*.

Directly opposite the chapel is the **baptistery**, where a plaque records the baptism of the six American natives brought back by Columbus from the New World in 1493. The stained glass above, representing *Christ and Mary Magdalene*, was executed by Gil Fontamet to designs by the great artist Bartolomé Bermejo from Cordoba.

CHOIR The central enclosed choir, which was begun after 1390, features some of the most impressive sculptural work to be found in the Cathedral. The original stalls were the upper ones, which were completed in 1399. The elaborate Plateresque canopies were added in the late 15c. Also added later were the coats of arms painted on the stalls by Juan de Borgoña on the occasion of the celebration here of the first and last chapter of the Order of the Golden Fleece in 1519. The meeting, presided over by the emperor Charles V - the Grand Master of the Order - was attended by the kings of England, Poland, Portugal, Denmark, Hungary and France. The coat of arms of England's Henry VIII is immediately to the right of the emperor's, facing the high altar.

The Cathedral

The lower stalls were executed by Macià Bonafè in 1456-62. The dazzlingly elaborate wooden *pulpit* (1403) by Pere ça Anglada is adorned with a traceried ironwork balustrade incorporating lily motifs. The splendid Renaissance *choir screen* was begun in 1519 by Bartolomé Ordoñez and completed in 1564 by Pedro Villar. Ordoñez himself was responsible for the exquisitely worked Italianate *reliefs of Sant Sever*, *Santa Eulàlia* and the scenes of Santa Eulàlia's proclamation of her faith and martyrdom at the stake.

SARCOPHAGUS OF SANTA EULÀLIA Between the choir and the presbytery steps lead down to the crypt chapel, which contains the most venerated object in the Cathedral: a *sarcophagus* containing the remains of the 4c co-patroness of the city, Santa Eulàlia. It is a particularly fine alabaster work of 1327, intricately carved by a Pisan artist who clearly had a close knowledge of the work of Giovanni Pisano. The previous sarcophagus - made immediately after the discovery of the remains in 877 - is now on the wall at the back of the crypt. Radiating like a sun in the middle of the star-shaped vault is a huge boss of 1371, carved with a relief of *Santa Eulàlia and the Madonna and Child*.

The presbytery was radically altered in 1970, when the 14c Bishop's chair was moved from the side to a central position at the rear. To accommodate this change the 14c gilded reredos above the high altar was taken away to the church of San Jaume, leaving an uninspired bronze by Frederic Marès of the *Exaltation of the Holy Cross* as the main embellishment. The ambulatory contains the wooden sarcophagi of Ramon Berenguer I, who died in 1025, and his wife Almodis. The third apsidal chapel contains a retable of 1450 by Bernat Martorell, with heavily gilded scenes representing the *Life of Christ*. When heading from the altar area towards the entrance to the cloister, you will see two ancient caskets suspended on the wall. By tradition they are considered the resting places of Count Ramon Berenguer I (1035-76) and his wife Almondis, but in fact they hold the remains of Petronila, the Aragonese queen whose marriage to Ramon Berenguer IV in 1149 united Aragon with Catalonia, and that of an earlier count.

The Cathedral cloisters

CLOISTERS Though begun by Bernat Roca in the late 14c, the cloisters were not completed until the late 15c, and have much Flamboyant Gothic detailing, such as the ironwork grilles entwined with floral motifs. The luxuriant character of the cloisters is due above all to the rich vegetation in the centre, featuring orange trees, aloes and palms hovering over a large pool and fountain, home to a gaggle of geese. The fountain that feeds the Cathedral's pond is protected by a mid-15c tabernacle decorated inside with a boss representing *St George and the Dragon*.

MUSEUM Partially occupying the chapter house, displays include a 15c retable by Jaume Huguet painted for the Guild of Esparto Workers and Bartolomé Bermejo's signed and dated *Pietà* of 1490, which was formerly in the chapel of the nearby Casa de l'Ardiaca (Archdeacon's House). Bermejo, a Cordoban-born artist who worked mainly in Catalunya and Aragón, is regarded as one of the greatest painters of the so-called Hispano-Flemish School.

on route

Barcelona Head, Passeig Colon. Opposite the main post office Roy Lichtenstein's abstract sculpture was completed in 1992 for the city's Olympic Games. *M* Barceloneta

Capella d'en Marcus, Plaçeta Marcus, off C/Carders. Open occasionally. This tiny early 12c Romanesque chapel was once part of a large hospital complex and the site of Spain's first postal station. The interior has been remodelled and includes an unremarkable Neoclassical retable. *M* Jaume I

Casa de la Ciutat, Plaça Sant Jaume. Sun 10.00-13.30 only; *T* 934 027 000, www.bcn.es. The City Hall is worth visiting to see the late-14c Saló de Cent and the decoration of 1928 by Josep Maria Sert in the Saló de Les Cróniques. *M* Jaume I, Liceu

Col.legi d'Arquitectes, Plaça Nova 5. *T* 933 015 000, www.coac.net. The College of Architects holds temporary exhibitions and has an interesting programme of events. The linear murals on the frieze were designed by Picasso. Good shop and restaurant. *M* Jaume I

Lamps in the Plaça de Palau, Plaça de Palau. In this compact square, just south of Santa Maria del Mar, there are lamps designed to emulate Gaudí's light fixtures in the Plaça Reial (p 104). *M* Barceloneta

Museu Barbier-Mueller d'Art Precolombí, C/Montcada 12-14. Tues-Sat 10.00-18.00, Sun and PH 10.00-15.00; closed Mon; *T* 933 104 516. Important collection of Pre-Columbian art, which includes sculpture, textiles, ritual objects and ceramics, from Central and South America. Shop. *M* Jaume I

Museu de la Xocolata, Antiguo Convent de San Agustín, C/Comerç 36. Tues-Sat 10.00-19.00, Sun and PH 10.00-15.00; *T* 932 687 878, www.museudelaxocolata.com. Exhibits chart the history of chocolate, its arrival in Europe and how it came to be so popular. Café and shop. *M* Jaume I

Museu del Calçat, Plaça Sant Felip Neri 5. Tues-Sun 11.00-14.00; closed Mon; *T* 933 014 533. Catalan shoes from the medieval period up to the present day, as well as shoemaking equipment and footwear worn by famous people. *M* Jaume I

Museu d'Història de Catalunya, Plaça Pau Vila 3, Palau de Mar. Tues-Sat 10.00-19.00, Wed 10.00-20.00, Sun and PH 10.00-14.30; closed Mon; *T* 932 254 700. Displays chart the history of Catalunya from prehistoric times to the present day, using imaginative interactive devices to engage visitors of all ages. Temporary exhibitions. Shop and good rooftop café. *M* Barceloneta

Museu d'Història de la Ciutat, Plaça del Rei. Tues-Sat: Oct-May 10.00-14.00, 16.00-20.00, Sun and PH 10.00-15.00; June-Sept 10.00-20.00, Sun and ph 10.00-14.00; closed Mon; *T* 933 151 111. In situ excavations of the Roman city, comprising streets, baths and the foundations of houses and shops. Maps, diagrams, models and photographs chart the history of the city. The museum also gives access to the apse of the Capella de Santa Agüeda, providing a close-up view of the magnificent altarpiece by Jaume Huguet. Book and gift shop. *M* Jaume I

Museu Diocesà, Av. de la Catedral 4. Tues-Sat 10.00-14.00 and 17.00-20.00, Sun 11.00-14.00; closed Mon; *T* 933 152 213. Housed in part of the Roman walls. Paintings, sculpture, textiles and ceramics from Barcelona churches. There are several noteworthy Romanesque church murals. Temporary exhibitions highlight different aspects of the collections. Gift shop. *M* Jaume I

Museu Frederic Marès, Plaça de Sant Iu 5 & 6. 10.00-19.00, Sun and PH 10.00-15.00; closed Mon; *T* 933 105 800, www.museumares.bcn.es. Collections of the sculptor and collector Frederic Marès (1893-1991), housed in a 13c Bishop's Palace. Paintings, sculpture, archaeological finds, toys, jewellery and much more. Courtyard café in summer. *M* Jaume I

Museu Tèxtil i d'Indumentària, C/Montcada 12-14. Tues-Sat 10.00-18.00, Sun and PH 10.00-15.00; closed Mon; *T* 933 197 603, www.museutextil.bcn.es. Fashion and textile collections housed in 14c mansion. Displays include 3c Coptic fabrics, Flemish tapestries and designs by Balenciaga and Azzedine Alaia. Courtyard café and shop. *M* Jaume I

Sala Montcada, C/Montcada 14. Tues-Sat 11.00-15.00, 16.00-20.00, Sun and PH 11.00-15.00; closed Mon; *T* 902 223 040. Run by the Fundació La Caixa, which holds outstanding temporary exhibitions by mainly contemporary Spanish and international artists. *M* Jaume I

Sant Pere de les Puel.les, Plaça de Sant Pere. Open for Mass daily. One of Barcelona's oldest parish churches, dating from the early 10c, and home to an order of nuns since the Middle Ages. The building was badly damaged in the Civil War and the subsequent reconstruction jumbled the architectural elements in defiance of any historical or artistic rationale. But the 12c cruciform interior remains intact. *M* Arc de Triomf

Santa Maria del Mar

Santa Maria del Mar, Plaça de Santa Maria. Mon-Sat 9.00-13.30, 16.30-20.00, Sun 10.00-13.30, 16.30-20.00; *T* 933 102 390. Magnificent church of cathedral-like proportions and one of the most eloquent examples of the Catalan Gothic style. Building began in 1329, and was completed in under 50 years. The interior was gutted by fire during the Civil War, which accentuates the extraordinary harmony and spaciousness of the architecture, enhanced by the wealth of 15c to 18c stained glass. *M* Jaume I

Taller Cuixart, Placeta Montcada 7. Tues-Sat 10.00-14.00, 17.00-20.00, Sun 10.00-14.00; closed Mon; *T* 933 191 947, www.cuixart.org. Changing exhibitions chart the development of renowned artist Modest Cuixart. *M* Jaume I

commercial galleries

Most galleries are open Tues-Sat 10.00-14.00 and 17.00-20.30.

Antonio de Barnola, C/Palau 4, *T* 934 122 214. Contemporary art by emerging and established Spanish and international artists. Also holds architectural and photographic exhibitions. Artists include Mireya Masó and José Manuel Ballester. *M* Jaume I

Maeght, C/Montcada 25, *T* 933 104 245, www.maeght.com. Housed in a 16c mansion and run by the people who created the famous gallery in Paris and the art foundation in St Paul de Vence. Artists include Joan Miró. Antoni Tàpies and Eduardo Chillida. *M* Jaume I

Metrónom, Fusina 9, *T* 932 684 298. Conceptual art, photography, concerts and dance events at this lively space run by collector Rafael Tous. *M* Arc de Triomf, Jaume I

eating and drinking

AT THE MUSEUMS

€   **Museu Picasso**, *T* 933 196 310. The café is surprisingly quiet, given the perpetual crowd inside. Sit outside or inside in an airy space with open brickwork. Sandwiches, salads, children's menu and speciality teas.

SURROUNDING AREA

€   **Antic Bocoi del Gòtic**, Baixada de Viladecols 3, *T* 933 105 067. In a medieval building adjoining the Roman city wall, come here to try *coca*, the Catalan version of pizza. *M* Jaume I

Arc Café, C/Carabassa 19, *T* 933 025 204. Thai and vegetarian food. Good for late breakfasts, lunch or dinner, or just a cocktail. *M* Drassanes

El Económico, Plaça San Agustí el Vell 13, *T* 933 196 494.

Unpretentious diner off the tourist beat. Good for a bargain lunch.
M Arc de Triomf

El Portalón, C/Banys Nous 20, *T* 933 021 187. Wonderful old *bodega*
in business since the 1860s. Wines from the barrel. *M* Liceu

Gente de Pasta, Passeig Picasso 10, *T* 932 687 017. Great salads,
pasta and risottos in designer setting. Open until 3.00 at weekends
for drinks with guest DJs. *M* Arc de Triomf

Habana Vieja, C/Banys Vells 2, *T* 932 682 504. Authentic Cuban
restaurant hidden away in an alley near the Picasso Museum.
M Jaume I

La Cerería, Baixada de Sant Miquel 3-5, *T* 933 018 510. Characterful
café specializing in milkshakes, ice cream and tea. Mostly
vegetarian food and good breakfasts. *M* Liceu, Jaume I

La Flauta Mágica, C/Banys Vells 18, *T* 932 684 694. Upmarket, mainly
vegetarian restaurant serving creative cuisine, with some organic
meat dishes also served. Open for dinner only. Booking essential.
M Jaume I

Café in the Barri Gòtic

La Locanda, C/Dr. Joaquim Pou 4, *T* 933 174 609. Authentic Italian cuisine with homemade pasta and pizzas baked in wood oven. Near Cathedral. *M* Catalunya

La Verónica, C/Avinyó 30, *T* 934 121 122. Situated between the boutiques and bars on the groovy Carrer Avinyó, with outdoor tables on Plaza George Orwell. Great pizzas, salads and desserts. *M* Liceu

La Vinya del Senyor, Plaça Santa Maria 5, *T* 933 103 379. Tiny bar in medieval building with lots of outdoor tables by Santa Maria church. Excellent selection of wines, many available by the glass, accompanied by Catalan specialities. *M* Jaume I

L'Hivernacle, Ciutadella Park, Passeig de Picasso, *T* 932 954 017. Beautiful café with Mediterranean and Japanese food in former hothouse. *M* Arc de Triomf

Living, C/Capellans 9, *T* 934 121 370. Fun restaurant and bar in former public laundry near the Cathedral. Outdoor tables, seasonal fusion cuisine and guest DJs. *M* Catalunya

Margarita Blue, C/Josep Anselm Clavé 6, *T* 933 177 176. Funky restaurant and bar with TexMex food. Becomes a crowded music bar after 21.00. Open late. *M* Drassanes

Oolong, C/Gignàs 25, *T* 933 151 259. Imaginative dishes drawing from many cuisines. Plenty of vegetarian options. Exhibitions. *M* Jaume I

Ovni, Via Laietana 32, *T* 933 107 756. Self-service vegetarian buffet with bargain set-price menus. Near Cathedral and Picasso Museum. *M* Jaume I

Slokai, C/Palau 5, *T* 933 179 094. Stables converted into funky restaurant with good soups and salads. *M* Jaume I, Liceu

Tèxtil Café, C/Montcada 12, *T* 932 682 598. At the entrance to the Textile Museum with tables in a medieval courtyard, this is an atmospheric spot for breakfast, lunch or just a drink. *M* Jaume I

Xocoa, C/Petritxol 11, *T* 933 011 197. Café with excellent hot chocolate, cakes and sandwiches. *M* Liceu

€€ **Agut**, C/Gignàs 16, *T* 933 151 709. Traditional Catalan food in renowned restaurant opened in 1924. *M* Jaume I

Ateneu Gastronòmic, Plaça Sant Miquel 2, *T* 933 021 198, www.ateneu.com. The imaginative Mediterranean menu offers unusual combinations at very reasonable prices. *M* Jaume I

Cal Pep, Plaça de les Olles 8, *T* 933 107 961, www.calpep.net. Terrific bar with daily specials (mostly seafood) cooked by Pep Manubens and his team. At lunchtime, try to arrive at one o'clock, just as it opens, to get a seat at the counter. *M* Jaume I, Barceloneta

Col.legi d'Arquitectes, Plaça Nova 5, *T* 933 015 000. Only open Mon-Fri 8.00-17.00. In the basement of the architecture school, this is a real find with a menu of creative cuisine that changes daily. Also good for breakfast. *M* Catalunya

Cometacinc, C/Cometa 5, *T* 933 101 558. Fusion cuisine with good salads in atmospheric space in medieval building. *M* Jaume I

Coses de Menjar, Pla del Palau 7, *T* 933 106 001. Quirky décor and unusual Mediterranean cuisine. *M* Jaume I, Barceloneta

Els Quatre Gats, C/Montió 3, *T* 933 024 140, www.4gats.com. Founded in 1897 in historic Modernista building. Once frequented by Picasso and other artists. Good for snacks or full meals. Live music in the evenings. *M* Urquinaona

Espai Sucre, C/Princesa 53, *T* 932 681 630. Unique restaurant that specializes in desserts, mixing sweet and savoury ingredients with surprising results. The taster menu is a real experience. *M* Jaume I

Estrella de Plata, Pla de Palau 9 and 13, *T* 932 680 635. Renowned gourmet tapas bar and restaurant. *M* Jaume I, Barceloneta

Little Italy, C/Rec 30, *T* 933 197 973. New York style Italian restaurant with live jazz on Wednesdays and Thursdays. Seasonal menu with vegetarian options and good wine list. *M* Arc de Triomf

L'Oucomballa, C/Banys Vells 20, *T* 933 105 378. Open evenings only. In a medieval building near the Picasso Museum. Interesting Mediterranean dishes with Oriental influences. *M* Jaume I

Pla, C/Bellafila 5, *T* 934 126 552. Open evenings only. Romantic hideaway in the heart of the Gothic Quarter. Seasonal Mediterranean cuisine with vegetarian options. *M* Jaume I

Salero, C/Rec 60, *T* 933 198 022. The imaginative food at reasonable prices, relaxed atmosphere and stylish white décor attracts an arty crowd. Open late for drinks. *M* Jaume I

Santa Maria, C/Comerç 17, *T* 933 151 227. Chic but informal bar with plenty of tables and an imaginative menu of gourmet tapas. *M* Arc de Triomf

Senyor Parellada, C/Argenteria 37, *T* 933 105 094. Authentic Catalan cuisine with a creative twist in 18c building with open-brick walls. Justifiably, a real local favourite. *M* Jaume I

Set Portes, Passeig de Isabel II 14, *T* 933 193 033, www.7portes.com. Founded in 1836, this huge, traditional restaurant specializes in rice dishes. Although touristy, popular with locals too. *M* Barceloneta

Shunka, C/Sagristans 5, *T* 934 124 991. Authentic Japanese food near the Cathedral. *M* Catalunya

€€€ **Abac**, C/Rec 79-89, *T* 933 196 600. Renowned chef Xavier Pellicer's chic restaurant in the Hotel Park is one of the best in Barcelona. Separate room to enjoy a cigar with coffee. *M* Jaume I, Barceloneta

Comerç 24, C/Comerç 24, *T* 933 192 102. Gourmet tapas created by top chef Carles Abellán, who previously worked at El Bulli. Taster menu recommended. Smoking discouraged. *M* Jaume I

Passadis d'en Pep, Plaça Palau 2, *T* 933 101 021. Chic yet relaxed restaurant run by the legendary Pep Manuben. Exquisite seafood and other delicacies. Hidden away down a corridor next to La Caixa bank. *M* Jaume I or Barceloneta

Pou Dolç, Baixada de Sant Miquel 6, *T* 934 120 579. Elegant décor and superior creative cuisine by top chefs. *M* Liceu, Jaume I

Torre de Altamar, Passeig Joan de Borbó 88, *T* 932 210 007. In the Torre Sebastià on the quayside, at a height of 75 metres with panoramic views. Creative Mediterranean cuisine. *M* Barceloneta

BARS & CLUBS

Café Royale, C/Nou de Zurbano 3, *T* 934 121 433. Chic bar with R&B, Latin and jazz music. *M* Liceu

El Ascensor, C/Bellafila 3, *T* 933 185 347. Cocktail bar with Modernista décor. *M* Jaume I

Ginger, C/Palma de Sant Just 1, *T* 933 105 309. Stylish cocktail and wine bar. *M* Jaume I

L'Angel, C/Gignàs 7, *T* 933 150 756. Popular bar with live jazz, blues and flamenco. *M* Jaume I

Luz de Luna, C/Comerç 21, *T* 933 107 542. Open until at least 4.00. Lively salsa club with spectacular dancing. *M* Barceloneta, Arc de Triomf

shopping

ACCESSORIES

Atalanta Manufactura, Passeig del Born 10, *T* 932 683 702. Handpainted scarves and textiles with quirky patterns. *M* Jaume I

Sombrereria Obach, C/Call 2, *T* 933 184 094. Berets and all sorts of hats. *M* Liceu

Sombrereria Mil 08010, C/Fontanella 20, *T* 933 018 491. Wide range of traditional hats and caps. *M* Urquinaona

ANTIQUES

Artur Ramon, C/Palla 10, 23 & 25, *T* 933 025 970. Three shops on the same street, specializing in paintings, engravings, drawings furniture and ceramics. *M* Liceu

L'Arca de l'Avia, C/dels Banys Nous 20, *T* 933 021 598. Antique silk, lace and linen. *M* Liceu

Maria Esclesans, C/Pietat 10, *T* 933 150 258. Barcelona's first antiques shop, founded in 1917. *M* Jaume I

BOOKS

Antinovs, C/Josep Anselm Clavé 6, *T* 933 019 070. Gay and lesbian bookshop with café, exhibitions and events. *M* Drassanes

Antoni Gabernet, Passatge Duc de Victòria 7, *T* 933 020 082, www.libreriagabernet.com. Huge range of antique books. *M* Catalunya

Cómplices, C/Cervantes 2, *T* 934 127 283. Gay and lesbian books, videos and magazines. *M* Liceu

Jordi Capell, Pl. Nova 5, *T* 934 813 562. Architecture and design books and magazines. Also architectural materials and equipment, furniture, lighting and objects by Catalan and international designers. *M* Liceu, Jaume I

Librería Maeght, C/Montcada 25, *T* 932 682 596. Art, photography, design and architecture books. *M* Jaume I

Pròleg, C/Dagueria 13, *T* 933 192 425. Feminist bookshop and information centre with a programme of cultural activities. *M* Jaume I

CLOTHES

Custo, Plaça de les Olles 7 and C/Ferran 36. **T** 932 687 893, www.custo-barcelona.com. Coveted patterned tops by Barcelona designer Custodi Dalmau. **M** Jaume I

GO30 Stocks, C/Vigatans 2, **T** 933 103 470. Last season's stock by top Spanish designers at bargain prices. **M** Jaume I

La Comercial, C/Rec 52, **T** 933 193 463, and 73, **T** 933 192 435. Stocks Amaya Arzuaga and Jocomomola, the diffusion line by top Spanish designer Sybilla. **M** Jaume I

Loft, C/Avinyó 22 and C/Boters 15, **T** 933 012 420. Stocks Vivienne Westwood, Helmut Lang and Jean Paul Gaultier. **M** Liceu

Natalie Capell, C/Banys Vells 4. Beautiful, unusual clothes by Israeli designer. **M** Jaume I

On Land, C/Princesa 25, **T** 933 100 211. Showcase for Barcelona designers, including Josep Font. **M** Jaume I

Overales & Bluyines, C/Rec 65, **T** 933 192 976. Top international designers plus second-hand section. **M** Jaume I

Tribu, C/Avinyó 12, **T** 933 186 510. Top labels including Diesel. **M** Liceu

CIGARS

L'Estanc de Via Laietana, Via Laietana 4, **T** 933 101 034. Wide range of tobacco, cigars and accessories. **M** Jaume I

CRAFTS

Antiga Pasamaneria J. Soler, Plaça del Pi 2, **T** 933 186 493. All manner of tassels, ribbons and cords. Founded in 1898. **M** Liceu

Arlequí Màscares, C/Princesa 7, **T** 932 682 752. Carnival, theatrical and comic masks. **M** Jaume I

Coral Bells Oficis, C/de la Palla 15, **T** 934 121 668. Jewellery, objects and fabrics made by local artists. **M** Liceu

Joan Piera, C/Cardenal Casañas 13, **T** 933 016 680, www.joanpiera.com. Art and graphic design materials. **M** Liceu

Popul-art, C/Montcada 22, **T** 933 107 849. Unusual contemporary ceramics made by local artists. **M** Jaume I

FOOD

Caelum, C/de la Palla 8, *T* 933 026 993. Cheeses, biscuits, teas and other products made at convents and monasteries around Spain. *M* Liceu, Jaume I

Casa Gispert, C/Sombrerers 23, *T* 933 197 535. Roasts almonds and other locally-grown nuts in traditional wood-burning oven. Also good for chocolate, olive oil and other gourmet products. *M* Jaume I

La Botifarreria de Santa Maria, C/Santa Maria 4, *T* 933 199 123. Top-quality charcuterie and cheeses. *M* Jaume I

Orígens 99.9%, C/Vidreria 6-8, *T* 933 107 531. Catalan gourmet specialities, including olive oil and wine. *M* Jaume I

Planelles-Donat, C/Cucurulla 9 and Av. Portal de l'Angel 7 & 25, *T* 933 173 439. Traditional place to buy *turrón* nougat. Open for more than two centuries. *M* Catalunya.

Tot Formatge, Passeig del Born 13, *T* 933 195 375. Wide range of Catalan and Spanish cheeses. *M* Jaume I

HOME & DESIGN

Cereria Abella, C/Boters 5, *T* 933 180 841. Traditional and contemporary candles by designers including Mariscal, Sybilla and Toni Miró. *M* Liceu

Cereria Subirà, Baixada Llibreteria 7, *T* 933 152 606. Founded in 1761, this candle specialist is the oldest shop in Barcelona. *M* Jaume I

Gotham, C/Cervantes 7, *T* 934 124 647. Furniture, lamps, etc, from the 1950s onwards. *M* Liceu, Jaume I

Vitra, Plaça Comercial 5, *T* 932 687 219. Chairs by world-renowned designers. *M* Jaume I

JEWELLERY

Moska, C/Flassaders 42, *T* 933 101 701. Unusual jewellery and objects by local designers in historic building. *M* Jaume I

Platamundi, C/Montcada 11, Plaça Santa Maria and C/Portaferrissa 22, *T* 932 681 094. Distinctive contemporary pieces by Catalan and Spanish designers. *M* Jaume I

Silver Designer, C/Montcada 22, *T* 933 152 749. Jewellery by contemporary designers. *M* Jaume I

KIDS

Creacions Umbert, C/Cardenal Casañas 19, *T* 933 019 834. Specializes in embroidering children's names on bibs, towels etc. *M* Liceu

El Ingenio

Drap, C/del Pi 14, *T* 933 181 487. Specialists in dolls' houses and furniture. *M* Liceu

El Ingenio, C/Rauric 6, *T* 933 177 138. Papier mâché figures, masks and theatrical props. Shop founded in 1838. *M* Liceu

Policlínica de Bebés, Galeries aldà, C/Portaferrissa 22, *T* 933 176 554. All sorts of dolls and dolls' clothes. *M* Catalunya, Liceu

Travi, C/de n'Amargós 4, *T* 934 126 692. All sorts of puppets. *M* Catalunya

LINGERIE

Casa Ciutad, Av. Portal de l'Angel 14, *T* 933 170 433. Beautiful old lingerie shop founded in 1892. *M* Catalunya

MUSIC

Cantabile, C/Lledó 4-6, *T* 933 199 629. Opera and classical music. Exhibitions and other events. *M* Jaume I

Herrera Guitars, C/Marlet 6, *T* 933 026 666, www.herreraguitars.com. Acoustic and electric guitars and accessories. *M* Liceu, Jaume I

New-Phono, C/Ample 35-37, *T* 933 151 361. Second-hand musical instruments. *M* Drassanes

Verdes Records, C/Duc de la Victòria 5, *T* 933 019 177. Music, DJ equipment and audition booth. *M* Catalunya

PHOTOGRAPHY

Arpí, La Rambla dels Capuchins 38 & 40, *T* 933 017 404. Photographic equipment with expert advice. *M* Liceu

SHOES

Casas, C/Portaferrissa 25 & Av. Portal de l'Angel 40, *T* 933 018 990.

Latest shoe designs, including Camper. *M* Catalunya

Czar, Passeig del Born 20, *T* 933 107 222. Trainer specialist which stocks unusual makes and vintage lines. *M* Jaume I

Solé, C/Ample 7, *T* 933 016 984. Handmade shoes and espadrilles from all over Spain. Also specializes in large sizes. *M* Drassanes

Vialis, C/Vidreria 15, *T* 933 199 491. Funky shoes and boots by top Catalan label. *M* Jaume I

STATIONERY

Conesa, C/Petritxol 10, *T* 933 015 330. Funky writing paper, cards, notebooks and pens. *M* Liceu

WINE

La Catedral dels Vins I Caves, Pl. Ramon Berenguer el Gran 1, *T* 933 190 727. Enormous selection of wines and spirits. *M* Jaume I

Vila Viniteca, C/Agullers 7-9, *T* 932 683 227. Friendly wine shop where the staff will advise you if you wish. *M* Jaume I

MACBA AND THE RAVAL

To the southwest of the great avenue of the Ramblas lies the area known as the Raval. Originally a poor suburb, which developed in the 13c outside the city walls, it was eventually surrounded by its own fortifications. After languishing through Barcelona's centuries-long depression it came back to life during the 18c revival. By the 19c it had become the site of factories; with a few exceptions, the city's wealthy stuck to the Ribera area, before striking out for the Eixample. Throughout most of the 20c the Raval was a dangerous slum, the haunt of prostitutes, drug addicts and criminals, evoking for one local journalist a *barrio chino* (Chinatown), a nickname which persists to this day. In recent years the neighbourhood has been on the upturn, fuelled by rising real estate prices and an energetic campaign by the city council which included demolishing whole blocks of medieval slums and laying out a new pedestrian 'Rambla del Raval'. Change is coming slowly and there are still rough spots, but with its blend of the medieval, genuine bohemian and stylish contemporary, this is one of Barcelona's most intriguing neighbourhoods.

Museum of Contemporary Art (MACBA)

OPEN	25 Sept-24 June: Mon, Wed-Fri, 11.00-19.30, Sat 10.00-20.00, Sun and PH 10.00-15.00; 25 June-24 Sept: Mon, Wed-Fri 11.00-20.00, Sat 10.00-20.00, Sun and PH 10.00-15.00
CLOSED	Tues; 1/1, 25/12
CHARGES	All exhibitions: €7, €5.50 reduced admission; two exhibitions: €5.50, €4 reduced admission; one exhibition: €4, €3 reduced admission €3 for all visitors to all exhibitions on Wed Reduced admission for senior citizens and students Free with Articket. Barcelona Card and Bus Turístic discount Free to children under 14 years. Free access for all on 12 Feb, 18 May and 24 Sept
TELEPHONE	**934 120 810**
WWW.	**macba.es**
MAIN ENTRANCE	Plaça dels Àngels 1
DISABLED ACCESS	Yes
METRO	Catalunya or Universitat
SHOP	Book and gift shop with wide range of art, design and photography books as well as exhibition catalogues and guidebooks. Stylish jewellery and bags, prints, posters, stationery, toys and design objects

There are guided tours on Wed and Sat at 18.00 and Sun and PH at 12.00. There are usually two temporary exhibitions, and a programme of events which includes film, video, book launches, talks, workshops, courses and children's activities.

The Museum of Contemporary Art (MACBA) opened in 1995 and has acted as a catalyst for the rehabilitation of the rundown Raval area, which has undergone radical urban development since then. While the district still has its problems, galleries, shops, restaurants and bars are springing up around the museum, turning the Raval into one of the city's most cutting-edge neighbourhoods.

The museum shows selections of work from its permanent collection of more than 2000 works on a rotational basis, as well as curating and hosting major temporary exhibitions. It also plans to stage exhibitions at other sites around Barcelona, including the Convent dels Àngels opposite the museum on the other side of the square. It is also probable that one of the former textile mills in the Poblenou area by the sea will be remodelled to create a large exhibition space.

THE BUILDING

The MACBA site and the square in front of it were created following the demolition of part of the Casa de La Caritat, which was founded in the 14c as a convent for Franciscan nuns. The museum was designed by the American architect Richard Meier. The circular white foyer opens onto a glass and enamelled metal atrium with ramps linking the three floors and the basement. A curving tower punctuates the other end of the façade. Meier is known for his innovative use of light, and here natural light floods the exhibition areas on all the floors. The top floor has higher ceilings than the lower floors, and benefits most from direct overhead light. There are plans to extend the building, with a new entrance designed by the artist Dan Graham.

HIGHLIGHTS

Dau al Set, *Joc de Cartes*

Joan Brossa, *Poema-Objecte*

Antoni Tàpies, *Pintura Ocre*

Antonio Saura, *Hia*

Miguel Barceló, *La Pêche*

Tony Oursler, *Flamenco Figure*

The holdings comprise works from the Government of Catalunya, the Barcelona City Council and the MACBA Foundation, as well as long-term deposits from the Telefónica Foundation, the Onnasch Collection and Sandra Alvarez de Toledo. The collection

Museum of Contemporary Art (MACBA)

concentrates on art from the second half of the 20c onwards, with an emphasis on Catalan and Spanish artists.

1945-67 The museum contains some works from the 1920s and '30s, including pieces by Alexander Calder, Paul Klee, Joaquim

Torres García and Leandre Cristófol, but the collection really begins with art produced in the 1940s. There are works by the members of the creative group **Dau al Set**, who formed in 1948 and published an influential magazine. Figures involved included Modest Cuixart, Joan Josep Tharrats, Antoni Tàpies, Joan Ponç, Joan Brossa and Arnau Puig.

Joc de Cartes (1949), a collaborative work by four members of the Dau al Set collective - Brossa, Tàpies, Ponç and Cuixart - is based on four playing cards (intended to convey a sense of random chance) each painted with forms which show the influence of Klee and Miró on the group. In *Poema-Objecte* (1956) artist-poet Joan Brossa juxtaposes a broom and a stack of dominoes in order to evoke associations and ideas unrelated to the character of the two pieces themselves – a visual poem. Antoni Tàpies' *Pintura Ocre* (1959) is an important multi-textured and multi-levelled work - one of his *pinturas matèriques* - from the mixed-media artist's early experiments with abstraction.

Other artists working during this period include Lucio Fontana and Josep Guinovart, represented by *L'arbre* (1958). In 1957, another group formed in Madrid. Called **El Paso**, its members included Antonio Saura, Martín Chirino, Manolo Millares, Rafael Canogar, Luis Feitó and Manuel Viola. The Aragonese painter Antonio Saura was heavily influenced by artists such as Jackson Pollock and Jean Dubuffet. In *Hia* (1958), a dark and evocative piece of Abstract Expressionism, he focuses, as in so many of his works, on the form of a woman. The collection contains several of Basque artist Jorge Oteiza's cube sculptures from the 1950s, including *Desocupación no cúbica del epacio* (1958-9). At the end of the 1950s, Albert Ràfols-Casameda developed a constructivist abstract style, illustrated by *Construcció* and *Pintura número 2: homenatge a Miró* (1971).

1968-70s The collection contains works by the leading conceptual artists active in Catalunya in the 1970s, including Antoni Muntadas, Zush, Fina Miralles, Pere Noguera, Francesc Torres and Francesc Abad. Before he became involved in performance art and events, Barcelona artist Antoni Miralda was producing pieces such as *La Cité du Loisir* (1967) and *Projecte de món per a un jardí* (1969).

International artists include Bruce Nauman, Gerhard Richter, Robert Rauschenberg and Mario Merz. Work by Marcel Broodthaers includes *Museum-Museum* (1972) and *Le Manuscrit trouvé dans une bouteille* (1974). Dieter Roth is represented by several pieces, including *Schokoladenmeer* (1970).

1980s The strong collection from the last two decades contains work by Spanish artists Eduardo Chillida, Joan Hernández Pijuan, José Maria Sicilia, Frederic Amat, Miquel Barceló, José Manuel Broto and Perejaume. Ferran García-Sevilla is represented by *Sèrie Déus* (1981), which comprises 60 paintings and uses several different languages and styles to explore the cultures of the world. There are still lifes by the Mallorcan artist Miguel Barceló, including *Ball de la carn* (1994) and *Taula Paradiso* (1991). *La Pêche* (1984) was inspired by a stay in the south of Portugal and signalled a new dynamism in his style, while still looking back to earlier works influenced by his island home.

Sculptures by Susana Solano include the iron and steel *El Puente* (1986) and *Estació termal* (1987). Sergi Aguilar is represented by his large steel sculpture *Acero* (1986), and Jaume Plensa by the aluminium column *Multindus* (1990). There are two pieces by Juan Muñoz, *London Balcony* and *Popular Songs II*, both made in 1987. Basque sculptors Txomin Badiola and Pello Irazu are also represented.

International artists include Anselm Kiefer, A.R. Penck, Keith Haring, Jean-Michel Basquiat, Mike Kelley, Jean-Marc Bustamente, Craigie Horsfield, and Tony Cragg. There are two pieces by German artist Rosemarie Trockel, the knitted wool *Made in Western Germany* (1943) and the fabric, wood and iron sculpture *Untitled* (1988). Tony Oursler's *Flamenco Figure* (1994) conjures up the shattered modern self in an eerie mixed-media sculpture which features a film-looped performance by Oursler and a collaborator projected on to the white face of a figure exuding apathetic despair.

Michel Lin *IT Park July 31-August 21 1999* (part of the CCCB's 2003 exhibition of avant-garde design, Crossed)

CENTRE DE CULTURA CONTEMPORÀNIA

OPEN	21 June–21 Sept: Tues–Sat 11.00–20.00, Sun and PH 11.00–15.00 22 Sept–20 June: Tues, Thur, Fri 11.00–14.00 and 16.00–20.00, Wed and Sat 11.00–20.00, Sun and PH 11.00–19.00
CLOSED	Mon; 1/1, 25/12
CHARGES	€4; reduced price €3, Wed, and for senior citizens, unemployed and students. Free for under 16s
TELEPHONE	**933 064 100**
WWW.	**cccb.org**
MAIN ENTRANCE	C/Montalegre 5
METRO	Catalonia or Universitat

Café-restaurant and good shop. Guided tours: Tues–Fri at 18.00; Sat, Sun and PH at 11.30.

Next door to the MACBA you'll find Barcelona's centre of contemporary culture, the CCCB, a busy hub of artistic activity throughout the year. This imposing 18c building, part of which was demolished to make way for the MACBA, was originally known as the Casa de la Caritat - in the past it was both a workhouse and a lunatic asylum. It was remodelled in 1994, to open up an extensive

Centre de Cultura Contemporània Courtyard

gallery space and the splendid sgraffitto courtyard was restored. Walking through this courtyard you reach a second patio which connects to the MACBA and is home to a pleasant outdoor café. The CCCB has no permanent collection but hosts a continuous programme of concerts, films, dance, temporary exhibitions and music festivals, including Barcelona's well known Sònar electronic music fair (mid-June).

HOSPITAL DE LA SANTA CREU

OPEN	Open during daylight Mon-Sat. **La Capella**, Mon-Sat 12.00-14.00, 16.00-20.00, Sun and PH 11.00-14.00
CHARGES	Free admission
MAIN ENTRANCE	C/Hospital 56.
METRO	Liceu

Founded in 1401 by King Martin I, this remained Barcelona's main hospital until the opening of Domènech i Montaner's new Hospital de la Santa Creu i Sant Pau in the Eixample (p 16). It was at the heart of the seedy Raval, surrounded by streets with names such as Egipciàques ('the Egyptian women', or 'prostitutes'), and it still retains a roughness of character. Within its walls, full of foreboding, you'll find a broad courtyard with orange trees and a medieval fountain. When not presided over by drunks or vagrants, it makes a pleasant spot for a rest. Part of the building is an art academy, while the upper floor, which is contained in a magnificently voluminous Gothic hall, is the National Library of Catalonia. A separate entrance from C/Hospital leads into **La Capella**, the hospital chapel, which hosts temporary exhibitions by up and coming local artists.

   Leaving the courtyard on the far side, you'll come to the **Institute of Catalan Studies**, set in a renovated 18c palace with an exuberantly decorated patio (you can poke your head in for a look, Mon-Fri 10.00-19.00). Across from here, the Neoclassical Royal Academy of Medicine (1760) has long been deserted; there are plans to reopen in it in the near future, at which point visitors will be able to see its sumptuous oval dissection theatre.

Palau Güell

OPEN	Mon-Sat: Nov-Mar 10.00-18.00; Apr-Oct 10.00-20.00
CLOSED	Sun and PH
CHARGES	€3 full price, €1.50 reduced price for students and seniors citizens Free with Ruta del Modernisme voucher
TELEPHONE	933 173 974
MAIN ENTRANCE	C/Nou de la Rambla 3-5, off Rambla de los Caputxins
METRO	Liceu
SHOP	Gaudí books and souvenirs

Visits are by guided tours only. Numbers are limited, so it is worth getting tickets the day before.

The Palau Güell is one of the most important of Gaudí's earlier works. It was built in 1886-8 as the extension of the Rambla town house of the industrialist Eusebi Güell, coinciding with the intense and exciting years of architectural activity leading up to the Barcelona Universal Exhibition of 1888. Eusebi Güell, whom Gaudí had first met in 1878, supposedly said that he liked the building less and less the more it went up, to which the architect replied that he himself liked it more and more. If this is true, then Güell was almost certainly being flippant, for he was to remain the most faithful of Gaudí's patrons.

During and after the Civil War, the building served as a police barracks and prison. It later housed the Centre of Theatre Studies, with a museum devoted to the history of the Catalan theatre. At the same time sinister, mysterious and exotic, the palace provided the perfect setting for one of the key scenes in Antonioni's atmospheric thriller, *The Passenger* (1977), when the main character, played by Jack Nicholson, first sets eyes on Marie Schneider.

The Güell family

The family fortune had been initiated by Eusebi's father Joan Güell i Ferrer, who had spent his early years in Cuba. With the vast amount of money that he had made there, Joan was later able to establish his own business in Barcelona. Between 1836 and 1860, he managed to revolutionize the local textile and metallurgical industries. He later developed an interest in agriculture and was able to take advantage of the phylloxera epidemic in France to build up Catalan viticulture. The finances and social position of the family were further improved when Eusebi married the daughter of another self-made man - the future Marquis of Comillas - and acquired for himself the titles of count, viscount and baron.

EXTERIOR The palace was restored between 1989 and 1992 by Antoni González Moreno-Navarro and Pablo Carbó Berthold. The distinctly forbidding façade is made from stone from the Güell family's quarry at Garraf. Colour is limited to the exuberant ceramic decoration on the twisted chimneys, which are only just visible from street level. The most exciting features of the exterior are the two large parabolic arches that form the entrance. Gaudí loved this geometrical form, which clearly illustrated his expressive and highly personal interpretation of the Gothic style. The portal features elaborate ironwork, in which Eusebi Güell's initials are clearly discernible, and a medieval-inspired heraldic motif that reinforces the fortress-like nature of the façade.

INTERIOR From the moment you enter the darkened vestibule, you find yourself in a world where a suggestive use of light and space has taken over from rational, symmetrical planning, making for a highly theatrical experience. A central ramp winds down to the brick basement with fungiform capitals and columns. Originally used for horses and carriages, for a short time after the Civil War this became a much-feared place of detention when political prisoners were tortured there.

The main-floor rooms, where the public life of the palace took place, have dark wooden surfaces, Moorish-style screens, medieval-inspired coffering and exquisite ironwork highlighted in

Palau Güell Roof terrace

gilding. The central atrium is surrounded by mysterious screened galleries that rise three floors to a dome pierced by holes as in a Moorish bath. The rooms above the main floor were used as bedrooms, while at the top of the house are the unornamented servants' quarters.

ROOF TERRACE The guided tour ends up on the roof, which is a riot of twisted chimneys covered in ceramic fragments, earthenware, marble and vitrified sandstone. This decoration had been lost, but was restored in 1992 by a team of specialist artists. The earthenware originally came from the Pickman factory in Seville, and the same type was used in the restoration, with the addition of two features representative of the 1992 Olympics: the Cobi mascot designed by Mariscal and the Barcelona logo used that year.

GAUDÍ'S LAMPS IN PLAÇA REIAL
METRO   Liceu

As part of the 19c modernizations which saw avenues such as Via Laietana and Carrer Ferran/Jaume I plough through the medieval tangle of the old city, a broad new public square was built just off of the Ramblas in 1848. The Plaça Reial was designed in Italianate style by Francesc Daniel Molina and adorned with a fountain depicting the *Three Graces* at its centre. In 1878 it was decided to add lamp-posts, and the young Antoni Gaudí was commissioned to design them. Taking the thriving commerce of the city as his inspiration, he crowned the lamps with winged helmets to symbolize Mercury, the Roman god of merchants and traders. The square remains a wonderful respite from the bustle of the Ramblas and Old Town, although you should exercise caution if you are there after 2 o'clock in the morning.

SANT PAU DEL CAMP
OPEN   Mon–Sat 10.00-12.30 and 16.00-19.30
CHARGES   Free admission
MAIN ENTRANCE   C/Sant Pau 101
METRO   Paral.lel

This monastery church is Barcelona's most important surviving Romanesque monument. Its name, meaning 'of the field', refers to a period more than a thousand years ago when this area was farmland and outside the city limits. The earliest

Plaça Reial

mention of the church is connected with the burial here in 912 of Count Wilfred II of Barcelona, but two Merovingian-style capitals dating from the 7c and 8c, which can be seen in the doorway, are better indicators of the age of the church. The most dramatic episode in its history was undoubtedly its destruction in 985 during the course of al-Mansur's sack of Barcelona.

The little cruciform church, with its compact cloister (13c), both of which have now sunk far below the rising ground level, contains a collection of fine 12c carved capitals and polyfoil arches, while the crude animal and human forms on the 13c entrance are also worth a look.

on route

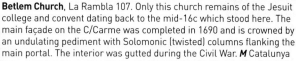

Betlem Church, La Rambla 107. Only this church remains of the Jesuit college and convent dating back to the mid-16c which stood here. The main façade on the C/Carme was completed in 1690 and is crowned by an undulating pediment with Solomonic (twisted) columns flanking the main portal. The interior was gutted during the Civil War. **M** Catalunya

Boqueria Market, La Rambla 105. Barcelona's spectacular main food market is housed in an exuberant mid-19c ironwork structure but there has been a market on the site for at least 700 years. From the exotic fruit stalls to the dazzling seafood section, strolling around provides a visual feast of the highest order. **M** Liceu

Centre d'Art Santa Mònica, La Rambla de Santa Mònica 7; **T** 933 162 810. Major contemporary art shows are held at this 18c converted convent, remodelled by Helios Piñón and Vicenç Viaplana. Excellent cultural information centre at ground level. **M** Drassanes

FNAC Triangle Open Mon-Sat 10.00-22.00. This modern shopping centre on the south side of Plaça de Catalunya features a continuous series of high-quality temporary photographic exhibitions. **M** Catalunya

Foment de les Arts Decoratives (FAD), Plaça dels Angels; **T** 934 437 520. Prestigious Catalan organization that promotes design and the decorative arts. Its annual awards are regarded as the benchmark of the Catalan design industry. Exhibitions, talks and other events. Bar and restaurant. **M** Catalunya, Liceu

Gran Teatre del Liceu, La Rambla 51-59; **T** 934 859 900, www.liceubarcelona.com. Barcelona's splendid opera house boasts state-of-the-art facilities with excellent acoustics following extensive remodelling after a fire in 1994. Built in 1847, it is one of the city's most important institutions. It has a seating capacity of 2338 and is one of the biggest opera houses in Europe. Part of the ceiling decoration is by leading conceptual artist Perejaume. The lavish interior may be visited on guided tours. Book downstairs in the Espai Liceu, which contains a large book, music and gift shop and a café. **M** Liceu

Hotel España, C/Sant Pau 9-11; **T** 933 181 758, www.hotelespanya.com. Late-19c hotel with ground floor designed by leading Modernista architect Domènech i Montaner in 1902-3. The two dining rooms retain a lot of the original furnishings, including elaborate ironwork candelabra. One of the rooms has extensive ceramic decorations, while the other is

Betlem Church

decorated with murals of mermaids by Ramon Casas. The bar has a fireplace sculpted by Eusebi Arnau. Good for lunch. *M* Liceu

Miró mosaic As you reach the centre of the Ramblas, at the point called the Plaça l'Ós, look down or you may miss the untitled abstract mosaic pavement by Joan Miró, one of the many public works that he made for the city. *M* Liceu

Museu de l'Eròtic, La Rambla 96bis. Open daily 11.00-21.00, €7; *T* 933 189 865, www.eroticamuseum.com. This surprisingly sophisticated little museum houses artifacts and exhibits relating to the physical side of human sexuality gathered from around the world, from ancient India to modern America. There are also regular temporary exhibitions of contemporary erotic art. *M* Catalunya, Liceu

Museu Marítim, Avinguda de les Drassanes. Mon-Sun 10.00-19.00, closed 1/1, 6/1, 25-26/12; *T* 933 429 920. The 13c Royal Shipyards house the Maritime Museum, the finest of its kind in the world. With its forest of enormous arches, the building is like a secular version of the Mosque in Cordoba. The imaginative displays chart Barcelona's long relationship with the sea and the history of the Royal Shipyards. There are models of the three ships that made the first voyage to America, together with the navigation instruments used. Shop and good restaurant. *M* Drassanes

Palau de la Virreina, La Rambla 99. Open Tues-Sat 11.00-20.30, Sun and PH 11.00-15.00; *T* 933 161 000, ww.bcn.es/cultura. Exhibition space run by the Barcelona Culture Department. Shows include contemporary art, design and photography. The building is an 18c palace with an elegant courtyard and traces of the original decoration. Book and gift shop. *M* Liceu, Catalunya

Sant Agustí, Plaça de Sant Agustí. The remains of the church of an Augustinian monastery built here in 1728. An example of the Catalan Baroque at its most austere, especially impressive is the unfinished façade with a porticoed atrium and giant Ionic columns. The interior lost most of its decoration in the Civil War. *M* Liceu

commercial galleries

Most galleries are open Tues-Sat 10.00-14.00 and 17.00-20.30.

ACC, C/Dr. Dou 7, *T* 933 176 906, www.ceramistescat.org. Exhibitions organized by the Association of Ceramicists of Catalunya. *M* Liceu, Catalunya

Art Petritxol, C/Petritxol 8, *T* 933 174 952, www.artpetritxol.com. 19c and 20c Catalan artists, including Nonell, Casas and Mir, as well as work by emerging artists. *M* Liceu

Cadakes Siglo XXI, C/Elisabets 2-4, *T* 933 010 318. Painting, graphic work, photography and new media. *M* Catalunya

Cotthem, C/Dr. Dou 15, *T* 932 701 669, www.cotthemgallery.com. Interesting space showing emerging and established artists including Jenny Holzer, Tony Oursler and Barbara Kruger. *M* Liceu, Catalunya

Dels Angels, C/Angels 16, *T* 934 125 454, www.galeriadelsangels.com. Painting, sculpture and photography by mainly Catalan artists. *M* Liceu

Doque, C/Joaquim Costa 47, *T* 933 021 477, www.doque.com. Work by emerging and established Latin American artists. *M* Universitat

Ego, C/Dr. Dou 11, *T* 933 023 698. Photography, installations, sculpture and painting by new Spanish artists. *M* Liceu, Catalunya

Espai Ras, C/Dr. Dou 10, *T* 934 127 199. Gallery and bookshop specializing in design and photography. *M* Liceu, Catalunya

Espai Vidre, C/dels Angels 8, *T* 933 189 833. Permanent and temporary exhibitions of contemporary glass objects. *M* Liceu, Catalunya

Estamperia d'Art, Plaça del Pi 1, *T* 933 186 830. Reproductions of old masters and contemporary art. *M* Liceu

Ferran Cano, Plaça dels Angels 4, *T* 933 011 548. New work by young Catalan artists and foreign artists based in Barcelona, including Jeleton, Pedro Oliver and Ana Marin. *M* Universitat, Catalunya

Sala Parés, C/Petritxol 5, *T* 933 187 020, www.salapares.com. Pioneering gallery, founded in 1877. Picasso held his first exhibition here. Now concentrates on figurative work by established artists. *M* Liceu

Trama, C/Petritxol 8, *T* 933 174 877, www.salapares.com/galeriatrama. Under the same ownership as the Sala Parés, this space is used for contemporary exhibitions, including design, architecture, illustration and comic art. *M* Liceu

eating and drinking

AT THE MUSEUM

€ **Metrópoli**, CCCB, C/Montalegre 5, *T* 934 120 954. Bar and restaurant in the CCCB. Outdoor tables behind MACBA. Good fixed-price lunch. *M* Catalunya

SURROUNDING AREA

€ **Bar Ra**, Plaça de la Gardunya, *T* 933 014 163. Open all day from breakfast until late. Lively spot for a meal, a drink, or brunch on Sundays. Outdoor tables behind Boqueria market. *M* Liceu

Buenas Migas, Plaça Bonsuccés 6, *T* 933 183 708. Foccaccia baked on the premises with lots of tasty fillings. Other Italian dishes also available. *M* Catalunya

Ca l'Estevet, C/Valldonzella 46, *T* 933 024 186. Legendary restaurant lined with photos of the many artists, writers and bullfighters who have eaten traditional Catalan food here. *M* Catalunya

Carmelitas, C/Doctor Dou 1, *T* 934 124 684. Big windows, tiled floors and formica tables in what was once part of a convent. Fashionable but not flashy. Modern Catalan food. *M* Liceu

Celta, C/Mercè 16, *T* 933 150 006. Galician tapas bar. Try the octopus and Padrón peppers with Ribeiro wine. *M* Drassanes

El Gallo Kirko, C/Avinyó 19, *T* 933 010 280. Pakistani food in restaurant backing onto the Roman city wall. *M* Liceu, Jaume I

El Pla dels Angels, C/Ferlandina 23, *T* 933 294 047. Opposite the MACBA with outdoor tables. Quirky design inside. Mediterranean and Italian food with good salads. *M* Universitat

Elisabets, C/Elisabets 2, *T* 933 175 826. Popular local restaurant with homemade Catalan and Mediterranean food. *M* Catalunya

Granja de Gavà, C/Joaquim Costa 37, *T* 933 175 883. Friendly café with good food, exhibitions, poetry readings and concerts. *M* Universitat

Granja M. Viader, C/Xuclà 4-6, *T* 933 183 486. Traditional café with marble tables, famous for its hot chocolate and homemade dairy products. Open for more than 100 years. Good for breakfast. *M* Catalunya

Juicy Jones, C/Cardenal Casañas 7, *T* 933 024 330. Funky juice bar with tables in the back. Good selection of mostly vegan dishes on a daily-changing menu. *M* Liceu

L'Antic Forn, C/Pintor Fortuny 28, *T* 934 120 286. Popular unpretentious place with set menus for lunch and dinner. Catalan and Mediterranean dishes. *M* Catalunya, Liceu

L'Hortet, C/Pintor Fortuny 32, *T* 933 176 189. Vegetarian food with good-value daily set menu, pizzas and range of juices. *M* Catalunya, Liceu

La Plata, c/Mercè 28, *T* 933 151 009. Popular tapas bar famous for its sardines, anchovies and tomato, olive and onion salad. *M* Drassanes

Los Toreros, C/Xuclà 3-5, *T* 933 182 325. Tapas and meals in characterful traditional diner decorated with bullfighting paraphernalia. *M* Catalunya

Macrobiotic, C/Carme 74, *T* 934 426 986. Only open during the day. Macrobiotic vegetarian food. *M* Liceu

Mamacafé, C/Doctor Dou 10, *T* 933 012 940. Relaxed café with daily menu using fresh ingredients from the Boqueria market. Exhibitions. *M* Catalunya

Organic, C/Junta de Comerç 11, *T* 933 010 902. Light and spacious vegetarian restaurant with salad bar. *M* Liceu

Punjab, C/Joaquim Costa 1, *T* 934 433 899. Very popular no-frills restaurant with a menu of Pakistani specialities. *M* Sant Antoni

Riera, C/Joaquim Costa 30, *T* 934 433 293. Bangladeshi dishes at bargain prices. Lots of vegetarian options. *M* Sant Antoni

Romesco, C/Sant Pau 28, *T* 933 189 381. Unpretentious diner popular with art crowd. Good set lunch. *M* Liceu

Rita Blue, Plaça Sant Agustí 3, *T* 932 450 865. Mexican and Mediterranean food. Live music and performances. Outdoor tables. *M* Liceu

Sésamo, C/Sant Antoni Abat 52, *T* 934 416 411. Vegetarian café and restaurant which uses organic produce. Fresh juices and herbal teas. *M* Sant Antoni

Suzet, C/Tallers 69, *T* 933 184 724. Open 10.00-2.00. Restaurant and bar with cool contemporary décor, specializing in crêpes, galettes and salads. *M* Catalunya

Taxidermista, Plaça Reial 8, *T* 934 124 536. Lively bistro designed by Beth Galí under the arches of the Plaça Reial. Outdoor tables. Good for a meal or a drink. *M* Liceu

€€ **Biblioteca**, C/Junta de Comerç 25, *T* 934 126 221, www.biblioteca.com. Iñaki López is one of the most exciting young chefs in Barcelona. Minimalist yet warm setting. Also sells cookery books. *M* Liceu

Can Culleretes, C/Quintana 5, *T* 933 173 022. Founded in 1786, this very popular restaurant serves traditional Catalan dishes at reasonable prices in a series of old-fashioned dining rooms. *M* Liceu

Can Lluís, C/Cera 49, *T* 934 411 187. Award-winning, family-run restaurant which has always been popular with artists and writers. The set-price lunch is a real bargain. *M* Sant Antoni

Dostrece, C/Carme 40, *T* 933 017 306, www.dostrece.net. Open 11.00-3.00. Restaurant, bar and club on two floors. Fusion cuisine, cocktails, brunch on Sundays, live jazz and guest DJs. *M* Liceu

El Cafetí, C/Sant Rafael 18 and C/Hospital 99, *T* 933 292 419. Early 20c décor and furniture. Specializes in Mediterranean cuisine, especially rice dishes. *M* Liceu

La Casa de La Rioja, C/Peu de la Creu 8-10, *T* 934 433 363. La Rioja cultural centre, with a restaurant serving regional specialities and, of course, excellent wines. *M* Liceu, Sant Antoni

La Gardunya, C/Jerusalem 18, *T* 933 024 323. At the back of La Boqueria market, so expect seasonal dishes and the freshest fish. *M* Liceu

Lupino, C/Carme 33, *T* 934 123 697. Elegant, minimalist design attracts upmarket media clientele. Imaginative seasonal menu and attractive outdoor tables on square at rear. Bar open until 3.00. *M* Liceu

Pinotxo, La Boqueria market, *T* 933 171 731. Having lunch or a coffee at this stall to the right of the main market entrance is an essential Barcelona experience. *M* Liceu

Salsitas, C/Nou de la Rambla 22, *T* 933 180 840. Lively bar and restaurant with white tropical décor and salsa music. Salads, pasta and seasonal dishes. After midnight, it turns into a club. *M* Liceu

Silenus, C/Angels 8, **T** 933 022 680. Stylish yet laidback bar and restaurant popular with art crowd. Varied menu with lots of salads and good-value set lunch. Exhibitions. **M** Liceu

Sushi & News, C/Santa Mònica 2 **T** 933 185 857. Just off the Ramblas, lively, fashionable Japanese restaurant where you can eat sushi and sashimi at the bar or have a sit-down meal. **M** Drassanes

€€€ **Ca l'Isidre**, C/les Flors 12, **T** 934 411 139, www.isidre.mhp.es. A favourite of King Juan Carlos. Specializes in updated traditional recipes, using the best seasonal ingredients. Excellent wine list. **M** Paral.lel

Casa Leopoldo, C/San Rafael 24, **T** 934 413 014. Renowned traditional Catalan restaurant, founded in 1929. First-class fish, meat and stews. **M** Liceu

Colibrí, C/Riera Alta 33-35, **T** 934 432 306. High-quality seasonal cuisine created by renowned chef César Pastor. **M** Sant Antoni

BARS & CLUBS

Al Limón Negro, C/Escudellers Blancs 8, **T** 933 189 770. Popular place in nightlife hub off the Rambla. Light meals, live music and exhibitions. **M** Liceu

Almirall, C/Joaquín Costa 33, **T** 934 121 535. Open 19.00-3.00. Try a glass of absinthe at this neighbourhood establishment which has been open since 1860 and is Barcelona's oldest bar. **M** Universitat

Aurora, C/Aurora 7, **T** 934 223 044. Open 20.00-2.30. Open for more than 50 years but still going strong. Stand downstairs or sit upstairs if there is room. Occasional live music. **M** Sant Antoni, Liceu

Baghdad, C/Nou de la Rambla 103, **T** 934 420 777. Open every night. The most famous and last surviving of Barcelona's sex clubs, featuring live erotic acts and entertainment. **M** Paral.lel

Benidorm, C/Joaquim Costa 39, **T** 933 178 052. Open 19.00-2.00. Red velvet, gilt mirrors and music from the 1960s to the latest releases make this unpretentious club a popular venue. **M** Universitat, Catalunya

Boadas, C/Tallers 1, **T** 933 189 592. Open 12.00-3.00. Art Deco cocktail bar on the corner of the Ramblas. Haunt of Hemingway and Picasso. **M** Catalunya

Dot Light Club, C/Nou de Sant Francesc 7, *T* 933 027 026, www.dotlightclub.com. Busy bar with guest DJs and video screenings. *M* Drassanes

El Café que pone Muebles Navarro, C/Riera Baixa 4-6, *T* 607 188 096. Open from 18.00 until late. A funky and relaxed bar, popular with arty types and located in a former furniture store. *M* Sant Antoni, Liceu

El Cangrejo, C/Montserrat 9, *T* 933 012 978. Mon-Sat 19.00-3.00. Legendary cabaret featuring transexual and transvestite acts - the Raval in all its seedy glory. Free but first drink obligatory. *M* Drassanes

Gimlet, C/Rec 24, *T* 933 101 027. Classic cocktail bar for stylish drinks without deafening music. *M* Jaume I, Arc de Triomf

Harlem Jazz Club, C/Comtessa de Sobradiel 8, *T* 933 100 755. Famous venue with live jazz, blues and flamenco performances. *M* Liceu

La Confitería, C/Sant Pau 128, *T* 934 430 458. Open 19.00-3.00. Bar in Modernista former cake shop. Tapas, exhibitions and occasional live music. *M* Paral.lel

La Paloma, C/Tigre 27, *T* 933 016 897. Opened in 1902, this traditional dance hall turns into a club after midnight. *M* Universitat

London Bar, C/Nou de la Rambla 34, *T* 933 185 261. Bohemian Modernista bar with live music and performances. *M* Liceu

Marsella, C/Sant Pau 65, *T* 934 427 263. Open since 1865, Dalí and Picasso used to drink absinthe here. It's now a popular haunt of young foreign tourists. *M* Liceu

Milk, C/Nou de la Rambla 24, *T* 933 010 267. Open 22.00-3.00. Fashionable bar decorated all in white. Mixed gay clientele. DJs. *M* Liceu

Moog, C/Arc del Teatre 3, *T* 933 017 282. Popular if over-priced club for dancing or chilling out to top guest DJs. *M* Drassanes

Muy Buenas, C/Carme 63, *T* 934 425 053. Old neighbourhood bar with Modernista décor; occasional music nights. *M* Sant Antoni

Pastís, C/Santa Mònica 4, *T* 933 187 980. Tiny and slightly dingy Boho haunt, exuding the atmosphere of Paris between the wars. *M* Drassanes

Raval Bar, C/Doctor Dou 19, *T* 933 024 133. Open 20.00-3.00. Busy bar on two floors, popular with actors. Serves food. *M* Liceu

Sidecar, Plaça Reial 7, *T* 933 021 586. Bar, club, restaurant and pavement café. Live music. All ages. *M* Liceu

Síncopa, C/Avinyó 35, no telephone. Lively, friendly bar with mix of jazz, reggae and World music. *M* Liceu

Soniquete, C/Milans 5, no telephone. Open Thur-Sun. Lively flamenco joint. *M* Liceu

Casa Bruno Quadros La Rambla de los Caputxins

shopping

ACCESSORIES

Alonso, C/Santa Anna 27, *T* 933 176 085. Beautiful gloves and fans in
shop open for more than a century. *M* Catalunya

Nina Pawlowsky, C/Nou de Sant Francesc 17, *T* 934 125 267. Avant-garde
hat designs. *M* Liceu, Drassanes

Paraguas Rambla de las Flores, La Rambla 104, *T* 934 127 258.
Umbrellas, fans and walking sticks. *M* Liceu

ANTIQUES

Art & Antiques Pironti, C/Palla 3, *T* 933 176 542. Ceramics from
Catalunya, Talavera and Alcora. *M* Liceu

BOOKS

Biblioteca, C/Junta de Comerç 28, *T* 934 126 221. Cookery book
specialist. Also restaurant. *M* Liceu

Dokumenta, C/Cardenal Casañas 4, *T* 933 172 527. Novels, art books,
guidebooks and English section. *M* Liceu

Loring Art, C/Gravina 8, *T* 934 120 108, www.loring-art.com. Bookshop
specializing in art, design, architecture, photography and theatre.
M Universitat.

Quera, C/Petritxol 2, *T* 933 180 743. Founded in 1916, specialists in
mountaineering, hiking and outdoor sports. *M* Liceu

Tartessos, C/Canuda 35, *T* 933 018 181. Specialist in photography, film
and art books. *M* Catalunya

CLOTHES

Comité, C/Notariat 8, *T* 933 176 883. Hidden-away boutique which
stocks clothes by new designers. *M* Catalunya

Defilo, C/Tallers 72, *T* 933 024 146. Unusual designs in silk and linen.
M Catalunya

El Chalet de los Alpes, C/Notariat 3, *T* 933 019 870. Shop and gallery
featuring work by young designers. *M* Catalunya

Giménez & Zuazo, C/Elisabets 20, *T* 934 123 381. Designer-run

boutique with clothes in unusual materials and colours.
M Catalunya

Lailo, C/Riera Baixa 20, *T* 934 4 3 749. Vintage clothes and accessories from all eras. *M* Liceu, Sant Antoni

Lucíanatural, C/Dr. Dou 9, *T* 934 122 911. Clothes, jewellery and accessories by Catalan designers. *M* Liceu, Catalunya

Moda Flamenca Flora Albaicín, C/Canuda 3, *T* 933 021 035. Flamenco dresses and accessories. *M* Catalunya

Recicla Recicla, C/Riera Baixa 13, *T* 606 110 118. Second-hand clothes, some from film and television productions. *M* Liceu, Sant Antoni

So Da, C/Avinyó 24, *T* 934 122 776. Shop and cocktail bar that stocks funky clubwear by top avant-garde designers. *M* Liceu

Spike, C/Hospital 46, *T* 934 126 467. Funky menswear and shoes by labels including Diesel, Petit Bateau and G-Star. *M* Liceu

Xancó Camiseria, La Rambla dels Caputxins 78-80, *T* 933 180 989. Shirt shop founded in 1820. *M* Liceu

CIGARS

Casa Gimeno, La Rambla 100, *T* 933 184 947. Amazing selection of cigars. *M* Liceu

FLOWERS

Llombart, C/del Pi 8, *T* 933 178 484. Founded in 1925, specializes in dried flower arrangements. *M* Liceu

FOOD

Biocenter, C/Pintor Fortuny 24, *T* 933 014 583. All sorts of health foods, organic fruit and vegetables, baby food and natural cosmetics. Also a restaurant. *M* Catalunya

Contemporary Food, C/Carme 66, *T* 934 427 327. Delicatessen with organic produce and specialities from all over the world. *M* Liceu

Escribà, La Rambla 83, *T* 933 016 027. The ornate Modernista façade is as exquisite as the cakes and chocolate on display inside. *M* Liceu

La Portorriqueña, C/Xuclà 25, *T* 933 173 438. Good quality coffee, roasted daily, including a great house blend. Also excellent hot chocolate made with cocoa beans from Brazil and Colombia. *M* Catalunya

Xocoa, C/Bot 4, **T** 933 188 991. Excellent chocolate in designer packaging. **M** Liceu

HOME & DESIGN

Cerería Abella, C/Sant Antoni Abat 9, **T** 934 410 907. Traditional candlemaker, in business since the 1860s. **M** Sant Antoni

Cerería Mas, C/Carme 3, **T** 933 170 438. Just off the Ramblas, this shop stocks a wide range of candles. **M** Liceu

El Indio, C/Carme 24, **T** 933 175 442. Draper's founded in 1870 with Modernista decoration featuring a mahogany hall, long counters and a black marble floor. **M** Liceu

Pan con Tomate, C/Dr. Dou 18, **T** 934 122 139. Furniture and household objects from the Far East and Africa. **M** Liceu, Catalunya

Trans.forma, C/Dr. Dou 16, **T** 933 018 905. Ceramics, sculptures and objects made by local artists. **M** Liceu, Catalunya

JEWELLERY

Forvm Ferlandina, C/Ferlandina 31, **T** 934 418 018, www.forvmjoies.com. Unusual jewellery by Spanish and foreign designers. Opposite MACBA museum. **M** Sant Antoni

KIDS

Joguines Foyé, C/Banys Nous 13, **T** 933 020 389. New and antique toys in century-old shop. **M** Liceu

La Lloca Dido, C/del Pi 8, **T** 933 105 538. Ragdolls, wooden toys and puppets. **M** Liceu

LINGERIE

Testimoni, Galeries Maldà, Plaça del Pi, **T** 934 121 529, www.testimoni.com. Designer men's underwear and beachwear. **M** Liceu

MUSIC

Casa Beethoven, La Rambla 97, **T** 933 014 826. Classical, Latin, pop and rock sheet music in shop founded in 1915. **M** Liceu

Casa Parramon, C/Carme 8, **T** 933 176 136. Makers of guitars and string instruments, open for more than a century. **M** Liceu

Castelló, C/Tallers 3,7 and 79, *T* 933
025 946. All sorts of music, plus
videos and DVDs. *M* Catalunya

Discos Edison's, C/Riera Baixa 9 and
10, *T* 934 419 674. Huge range
of second-hand records, CDs
and videos. *M* Sant Antoni

Etnomusic, C/Bonsuccés 6, *T* 933
011 884, www.etnomusic.com.
World music specialist.
M Catalunya

L'Art Guinardó, C/Tallers 67, *T* 933
185 095, www.artguinardo.com.
Electric guitars and
accessories. *M* Catalunya

Off, C/Nou de Sant Francesc 36,
T 933 180 857. Music for
clubbing and chilling out.
M Drassanes

Revolver, C/Tallers 13, *T* 933 021
685. New, used and imported
music. *M* Catalunya

Casa Beethoven

shop!

PHOTOGRAPHY

Casanova, C/Tallers 68 and C/Pelai 18, *T* 933 016 112. Wide range of
photographic equipment. Knowledgeable staff. *M* Catalunya

SHOES

Casas, La Rambla 125, *T* 933 024 598. Fashionable shoes by top Spanish
and international designers including Marc Jacobs, Dries van
Noten and Helmut Lang. *M* Catalunya

La Manual Alpargatera, C/Avinyó 7, *T* 933 010 172. Espadrilles from all
over Spain. Lots of celebrity customers. *M* Liceu

STATIONERY

Paperam, C/dels Àngels 4, *T* 933 181 890. Wide range of paper,
stationery and art materials. *M* Catalunya, Liceu

Raima, C/Comtal 27, *T* 933 174 966. Paper, diaries, notebooks, designer briefcases and bags. *M* Catalunya

Verkerke, C/Cardenal Casañas 12, *T* 933 020 186. All sorts of posters, reproductions and cards. *M* Liceu

TOYS

Casa Palau, C/Pelai 34, *T* 933 173 678. Everything for the train set fanatic, as well as Scalextric and model cars. *M* Catalunya, Universitat

WINE

El Celler de la Boqueria, C/Petxina 9, *T* 933 019 937, www.cellerboqueria.com. Wide selection of still and sparkling wines from Catalunya and the rest of Spain. Tastings, courses, talks and other events. *M* Liceu

MONTJUÏC

If the Old City is Gothic and the Eixample Modernista, Montjuïc, rising above the city south of the Old Town, is best typified as Noucentista. The hill, which rose up from the Mediterranean before modern land reclamation projects pushed the sea back, has been inhabited since ancient times, and has traditionally served as the city's cemetery, first in the Middle Ages for the Jewish population (hence the name, the Jewish hill). Until the early 20c Montjuïc was primarily a military installation, intended to protect but also to dominate the town. In 1929 a second Universal Exhibition was held in the city, centred on Montjuïc, with its elaborate fairgrounds constructed in Noucentista style. The area was further transformed by a series of renovation and infrastructure projects carried out in preparation for the 1992 Olympic games, the hosting of which put Barcelona back on the world stage. Montjuïc today is a centre for art and culture, with two major museums and several smaller ones on its slopes. The hillside also incorporates several city gardens, which are pleasant during the day but less salubrious at night; and it is still crowned by a military installation. You can reach Montjuïc by walking from Plaça d'Espanya, which has the best access to the MNAC, by a combination of funicular and chair-lift from Metro Paral.lel for access to the Fundació Miró and the castle, or by the cable-car from Barceloneta or the port, which takes you about halfway up and a considerable walk from any of the sights.

National Museum of Catalan Art (MNAC)

OPEN	Tues-Sat 10.00-19.00, 10.00-14.30 Sun and PH
CLOSED	Mon, 1/1, 1/5, 25/12
CHARGES	Permanent collections €4.80; temporary exhibitions €4.20. €10.40 for MNAC and Poble Espanyol combined Free with Articket. 20% discount with Barcelona Card or Bus Turístic. 30% discount for senior citizens, unemployed and students. Free first Thur of each month, 11/9, 24/9 and 18/5
TELEPHONE	**936 220 376/0360**
WWW.	**mnac.es**
MAIN ENTRANCE	Palau Nacional, Parc de Montjuïc
DISABLED ACCESS	Facilities including wheelchairs available
METRO	Espanya
SHOP	Wide range of art and guide books, cards, posters, prints and gifts
EATING	A new café is being installed

There is usually at least one temporary exhibition running. Guided tours.

The idea of creating a museum devoted to the fine arts in Barcelona goes back to the late 19c and was realized on the basis of works amassed during the World Exhibition of 1888. After 1907, work began on documenting the numerous Romanesque frescoes in the isolated churches of the Catalan Pyrenees. Many of these were removed from their original settings between 1919 and 1923 and are now displayed in rooms emulating the shapes of the churches from which they were taken. These unrivalled holdings of Catalan Romanesque art make this the finest museum of medieval art in Spain, if not in Europe. The extensive collection of Catalan Gothic art, which dates from the 13c-15c, was begun as part of the movement to preserve Catalunya's artistic heritage following the dissolution of religious foundations in 1835, and was augmented by the donation of several private collections.

In 1985 a complete re-organization of the museum's collections was begun, and the architects Gae Aulenti and Enric Steegmann were entrusted with the task of remodelling the interior of the Palau Nacional to enable more of the museum's holdings to be exhibited. Important new displays are scheduled to open in late 2004 and will comprise a more extensive installation of Renaissance and Baroque art, a photography section, and the collection of 19c and 20c art which is being transferred from the Museu d'Art Modern (p 69).

THE BUILDING

The Palau Nacional, built for the 1929 International Exhibition, was conceived by Puig i Cadafalch to act as the dominant element of the monumental vista leading from the Plaça d'Espanya down the Avinguda de la Reina Maria Cristina. His basic intentions were respected, though the structure was built using the designs of Enric Català i Català and Pedro Cendoya Oscoz. The end result was an eclectic structure of remarkable heaviness and pomposity, with elements derived from Spanish Baroque and Neoclassical architecture.

Palau National

The central hall was originally used for the official ceremonies connected with the International Exhibition. Its dome is painted with frescoes by Francesc Galí, Josep de Togores and Manuel Humbert, with sculptural decoration by Enric Casanovas and Josep Dunyach.

HIGHLIGHTS

ROMANESQUE
Madonna of Ger — Section IV

Murals from the church of Sant Climent de Taüll — Section V

Capitals from Camarasa and the Convent de Sant Francesc — Section VI

Frescoes from the church of Santa Maria de Taüll — Section VII

Batlló Christ in Majesty — Section VIII

GOTHIC
Altarpiece of St Barbara, **attributed to Gonçal Peris Sarrià** — Section VIII

Catalan International Gothic paintings and sculpture — Section IX

Altarpiece of St Vincent **by Bernat Martorell** — Section XI

St George and the Princess **by Jaume Huguet** — Section XII

The Romanesque, Gothic and Renaissance and Baroque collections are displayed on the ground floor. The 19c and 20c collection and the photography section will be displayed on the upper floor from late 2004. Temporary exhibitions are usually held in the basement.

MUSEU NACIONAL D'ART DE CATALUNYA

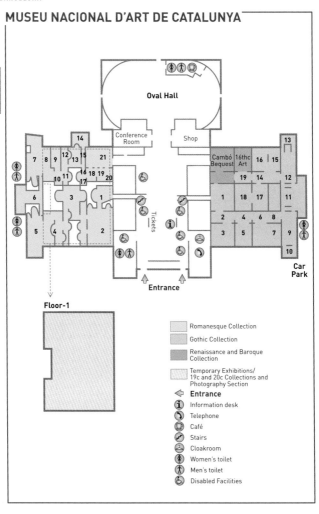

Oval Hall

Conference Room

Shop

Floor-1

Romanesque Collection

Gothic Collection

Renaissance and Baroque Collection

Temporary Exhibitions/ 19c and 20c Collections and Photography Section

◁ **Entrance**

ⓘ Information desk

☎ Telephone

☕ Café

⟳ Stairs

⬤ Cloakroom

♀ Women's toilet

♂ Men's toilet

♿ Disabled Facilities

Entrance

Tickets

Cambó Bequest

16thc Art

Car Park

ROMANESQUE ART

SECTION I The introductory space contains tombstones with Latin, Arabic and Hebrew inscriptions. The highlight is the beautiful early 12c *frontal of the Apostles* as well as Carolingian and Catalan coins, including the *mancús* gold coin minted by the Count of Barcelona in the 11c, which was inspired by the Islamic coins of Al-Andalus.

SECTION II The chronological displays begin with 11c paintings from the church of Sant Joan de Boí in the Alta Ribagorça area in the Pyrenees. The c 1100 mural of the *Stoning of St Stephen* was once part of a larger series depicting saints' lives and intended to illustrate the Bible to church-goers. The figures reveal the influence of classical and Byzantine art.

SECTION III is devoted to the Pedret Circle, with works from different churches by the **Master of Pedret** and his apprentices. Influenced by the style prevalent in late 11c northern Italy, these include a cycle from one of the side apses of the Mozarabic parish church at Sant Quirze de Pedret. The many winged and multiple-eyed seraphim from Santa Maria d'Àreu are striking, and the apsidal painting from El Burgal has an early donor portrait, that of Llucía, Countess of Pallars.

SECTION IV deals with Christ and the Madonna in iconography. The apses of Santa Maria de Mur and San Miguel de Marmellar both show the *Ascension of Christ*. The baldachin panel from Tost (c 1200) depicts *Christ in Majesty and the Tetramorph* (the tetramorph being an image that combines the symbolic attributes of the Evangelists) in a style that became more popular later in the century. The *Madonna of Ger*, a polychrome wood figure, is a key work of Catalan Romanesque art as it is one of a distinctive series which emerged in the second half of the 12c in the Pyrenees.

SECTION V Stairs lead down to some of the most outstanding exhibits: murals and liturgical furniture from the 12c Romanesque church of **Sant Climent de Taüll**, from the Boí Valley, which should also be viewed from the gallery at ground level. The central apse is dominated by a *Christ in Majesty* of mesmerizing power by the Master of Taüll. The expressiveness in the use of line, and the bold foreshortening and simplification of forms, reveal an artist of great individuality, and one who appears to have had a significant influence on the early development of both Picasso and Miró.

SECTION VI Back on the ground floor, this room takes up again the theme of Section I with displays of monumental sculpture from the 12c and 13c, mainly from the Pyrenees. One voussoir (a stone from an arch) from Ripoll features a helmeted man regurgitating a ram. There are reconstructed fragments of the delicate late-12c cloister of the church of **Sant Pere de les Puel.les** in Barcelona. An important ensemble of 13c pieces from the church of **Sant Miquel** at Camarasa Castle includes a pillar with a Corinthian capital carved with the figures of Adam and Eve with the serpent on one side and the Sacrifice of Isaac on the other. The early 13c carved capitals from the **Convent of Sant Francesc** (1200–20) are of special interest because they represent a transitional phase from Romanesque to Gothic. The sculptures may be the work of Master Mateo, famous for his work on the Cathedral of Santiago de Compostela; they indicate that Catalan art was influenced by northern Spanish techniques, itself strongly affected by new northern French styles.

SECTION VII You go downstairs again to see the 12c frescoes from the apse and wall of **Santa Maria de Taüll** in the Boí Valley, which should also be viewed from ground level. These are the most extensive and among the best preserved in the museum. The figure of Mary presides over the apse, while the side walls include scenes of the Three Wise Men and a remarkably realistic and gruesome portrayal of Hell. The wall facing the apse features David fighting with Goliath.

SECTION VIII This room displays 12c polychrome wooden sculpture, including a *Virgin and Child*, two figures from a *Descent from the Cross* and the magnificent *Batlló Christ in Majesty* (1147),

The Master of Taüll *Christ in Majesty* (12c)

one of the museum's masterpieces. It is a richly coloured work featuring a tunic adorned with Islamic motifs. The figure of Christ, which was restored in 1952, is exquisitely carved, particularly on the face and abdomen.

SECTION IX The paintings from the church in **Sorpe** feature scenes from the Old and New Testament, including the miracle of the catch of fish in the Sea of Galilee, depicted on the first triumphal arch. The intrados (the inner curve) of the arches feature martyred saints and signs of the zodiac.

SECTION X The martyrdom of saints is illustrated by the splendid 12c altar frontal from the church of **Sant Quirze and Santa Julita** in Durro in the Boí Valley. Thought to have been martyred in Tarsus in the 4c, St Cyricus and his mother, Julitta, are shown being sawn in half, stabbed with swords, boiled alive and having nails hammered into their heads.

SECTION XI The paintings from the churches in **Estaon** and **Surp**, dating from the second half of the 12c, are thought to have been executed by artists who had been taught by the great masters of the Pedret and Taüll churches. The fresco of *St John the Evangelist* from the church of Sant Iscle and Santa Victòria in Surp is similar in style to the work of the Master of the Last Judgement, who painted some of the scenes in the churches in Taüll (Section VII).

SECTION XII These Andorran murals date from the second half of the 12c, and depict Christ in Majesty surrounded by the Tetramorph.

SECTION XIII This room addresses the period c 1180-1230, when Byzantine influences brought about a renewal in Western art. The altar frontal from Baltarga may have been painted by a Greek or Byzantine artist and is notable for the almost sculptural quality of the figures.

SECTION XIV Turn left down a passage - which is actually Section XV - to access this room at the rear of the building. It contains paintings from the atrium of the Lombard-influenced church of

Sant Vicenç in Cardona Castle (1029-40). The paintings date from the second half of the 12c, apart from the *Defence of Girona*, which was painted after 1285 when the battle in question took place.

SECTION XV The metal and enamel work displayed here includes 13c censers and objects from Limoges, including the *Mondoñedo crozier* and a *Eucharistic Dove*.

SECTIONS XVI AND XVII The iconography of the 13c paintings from the apse of the church of **Sant Cristòfol** in Toses shows how Gothic influences were beginning to affect Romanesque style. The intrados of the apse window depicts the offerings of Cain and Abel. The second half of this section deals with angels in iconography.

SECTIONS XVIII-XXI The final room is divided into four parts. The first section contains other late-Romanesque 13c works and coins from the reign of Jaume I of Barcelona and Aragon. The next section displays works from the influential **Ribagorça workshop**, which is thought to have been based around the old Cathedral of Roda in the second half of the 13c. The end of the room displays fragments of mural paintings from the palatine hall of the Benedictine **Monastery of San Pedro in Arlanza** (c 1210), which depict mythical creatures and are linked stylistically to English miniature art.

The last section contains murals from the main chapter house of Sigena in Aragon, which are believed to have been painted c 1200 by English artists who had worked on the Winchester Bible and were familiar with Sicilian mosaics. Considered to be a masterpiece of neo-Byzantine art, the paintings were seriously damaged by fire in 1936.

GOTHIC ART
SECTION I The museum's holdings of Gothic civic art (13c-15c) are displayed here. Exhibits include murals depicting Jaume I's conquest of Mallorca in 1229, which were painted in 1285-90 and

come from the **Palau Caldes** in Barcelona's Carrer de Montcada, which is now part of the Picasso Museum.

SECTION II Gothic art in Aragon, Navarre and Castile in the late 13c and early 14c is represented by murals from the church of San Fructuosos in Bierge in the Sierra de Guara in Aragon. These works, notably the *Life of St Nicholas*, illustrate the transition from late Romanesque to Gothic.

SECTION III The objects in this room represent the definitive adoption of the Gothic style in Catalonia. A highlight is the richly decorated *reliquary chest of St Candidus* (1292).

SECTIONS IV-V The Catalan sculpture from the second half of the 14c and the early 15c displayed here reflects foreign influences. The sculptures of **Jaume Cascalls** (mid-14c) show an increasingly emotive naturalism; note especially the *Altarpiece of the Virgin Mary and St Anthony the Abbot* and the *Head of Christ*.

SECTION VI-VII Italianate influences were highly apparent in Catalunya in the early 14c, as shown by the work of Ferrer and Arnau Bassa. Ramon Destorrents, represented by a small panel of *St Matthias*, succeeded Ferrer Bassa as court painter and influenced the Serra brothers, who came to prominence in the second half of the 14c. Key works include **Pere Serra**'s *Madonna of the Angels and Saints* and **Jaume Serra**'s *Altarpiece of St Stephen*. The *Altarpiece Devoted to the Virgin* (c 1362-75) by the Master of Sigena is thought also to be by Pere Serra.

SECTION VIII Valencian International Gothic refers to the art of the turn of the 15c which embraced new ideas from France, Italy and the Netherlands and emerged strongly in the Valencia region, where several foreign artists were working. The towering *Altarpiece of St Barbara* (c 1410-25), attributed to **Gonçal Peris Sarrià**, is a splendid example of the International Gothic style.

SECTION IX Turn right into this large space which begins the displays of Catalan International Gothic and is one of the most important in the museum. One of the chief exponents was **Lluís Borrassà**, represented here by the semicircular *Retable of Guardiola* of 1404. Other highlights include the *La Seu d'Urgell Altarpiece of St Michael and St Peter* (1432-3) by Bernat Despuig and Jaume Cirera, and the *Altarpiece of St John the Baptist and St Stephen* (c 1445-53) which is attributed to Joan Antigó and Honorat Borrassà.

SECTION X This area at the end of Section IX contains the rich bequest of Pere Fontana i Almeda. The *Altarpiece of Saints Jerome, Martin of Tours, Sebastian and the Crucifixion* (c 1445-55), a large, four-panel retable by **Jaume Ferrer**, was probably painted for an Aragonese church. The distinctive composition in which portraits of the main protagonists dominate reflects a Humanistic trend more typical of Valencian and Mallorcan art than of Catalan Gothic painting of this period.

SECTION XI Retrace your steps through Section IX to the central area which is devoted to **Bernat Martorell** and **Lluís Dalmau**. Born c 1400, Martorell, who has been identified as the Master of Saint George, introduced new stylistic techniques and exerted a great influence on other Catalan artists. The *Altarpiece of St Vincent* (c 1435-40) is one of his finest works.

The work of Lluís Dalmau suggests that he was influenced by Flemish art: he is thought to have met Van Eyck. His masterpiece, the *Madonna of the Councillors*, was painted in 1443-5 for the chapel of Barcelona's Town Hall, and portrays the Madonna and Child flanked by the city councillors, and Sts Eulàlia and Andrew.

SECTION XII The next area concentrates on **Jaume Huguet** and his workshop, whose work here includes the sublime central panel of the *Triptych of St George and the Princess*, thought to date between 1459 and 1475. A stern St George, patron saint of Catalonia, in gilded armour, accepts an offering from the princess. The background landscape, featuring cypress trees, reflects the influence of the Italian Renaissance on Catalan painting of this period. A coat of arms on the back of the panel indicates that it is likely to have been commissioned by the powerful Cabrera family. The finest of the panels from the *Altarpiece of St Augustine* or *of the Tanners* is the elaborately-detailed Consecration, where the saint is depicted as a bishop in exquisite robes.

SECTION XIII This room at the far end of the space is devoted to **Pere Garcia de Benabarre** and the **Vergós family**. Benaberre's *Virgin and Four Angels* (c 1470) is one of his finest works from a prolific period in Lleida. The Vergós family from Barcelona were heavily influenced by Huguet, in whose workshop they were probably apprentices, and are represented here by 14 panels from the *Altarpiece of St Stephen* (1492-1500) from Granollers.

SECTION XIV The next set of rooms begins with the influence of Flemish art in Mallorca, Castile, Andalusia and Extremadura, from the second half of the 15c. The two key figures of this movement were **Fernando Gallego**, whose *Epiphany* (c 1480-90) is displayed here and the remarkably original Cordoban-born artist **Bartolomé Bermejo**. His *Resurrection and Descent of Christ into Limbo* (c 1480) shows the naked and realistically observed figure of Christ struggling against a chiaroscuro background of agitated bodies.

SECTION XV The compositions of the **Master of La Seu d'Urgell** herald the introduction of Renaissance elements into Catalan art in the last third of the 15c. The two compartments comprising the *Presentation of Jesus in the Temple* (c 1495) are from the organ doors of the Cathedral of La Seu d'Urgell.

SECTION XVI The Flemish influence on art in Valencia and Aragon is shown by an excellent group of paintings, which include a panel of *St Margaret and the Dragon* (c 1451-8), attributed to the Valencian artist Jacomart. Joan Reixac was a disciple of Jacomart and took on some of his commitments following the latter's death in 1461. He is represented by the *Altarpiece of the Epiphany* (c 1465) and the *Altarpiece of St Ursula* (1486).

SECTION XVII Crossing back through Section XIV brings you to

Jaume Huguet *Altarpiece of St Augustine* or *of the Tanners* (detail; late 15c)

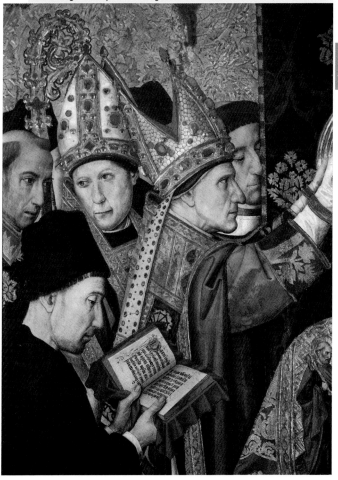

this large room which deals with the representation of the donor in mid-15c art. Gothic and Renaissance religious art was often commissioned by members of the high clergy or nobility who would then be featured in the work, typically kneeling in prayer, offering a donation to Christ, the Virgin or the saint in question. Highlights include Martín Bernat's *St Anthony Abbot and Donors* (1495) and the *Mass of St Gregory* (c 1480), which is attributed to Diego de la Cruz. This room also displays religious gold and silverware, including the *Chalice of Queen Maria de Luna* (1396-1406), which was made in Valencia and features cobalt blue and emerald green enamelling.

SECTION XVIII The displays of funerary art include two richly-decorated sarcophagi (c 1300) of members of the Téllez de Meneses family from Castile.

SECTION XIX The development of the representation of the Madonna in European sculpture is illustrated by a c 1400 *Madonna* by the Bohemian School and work from French and English workshops.

SECTION XX The 15c and 16c Flemish and Hispano Flemish art displayed here forms the beginning of the Renaissance and Baroque collection (see below), and includes the gruesome *Beheading of St Cucufate* (1504-7) by the northern-born Anye Bru, a work of expressive brutality recalling German paintings of this period.

RENAISSANCE AND BAROQUE ART
THE CAMBÓ BEQUEST

This collection will be fully installed in late 2004. Until then, the displays consist of works from the bequest of the financier and politician Francesc Cambó, which comprises European artists from the 16c-19c. Spanish painters include Zurbarán, Sánchez Coello, El Greco and Goya. Italian art is represented by Veronese, Tintoretto and Tiepolo, and Flemish art by Rubens, Quentin Metsys and Lucas Cranach the Elder.

19C AND 20C ART COLLECTION

The museum's important collection from this period is scheduled to be transferred from the Museu d'Art Modern (p 69) in 2004 and installed on the upper floor.

The collection begins with Marià Fortuny (1838-74), who is treated here as a precursor of Modernisme (the Catalan form of Art Nouveau) and was the first Catalan artist to achieve an international reputation.

The **Modernisme** displays start with the principal artists of the first generation of the movement, Ramon Casas (1866-1932) and Santiago Rusinyol (1861-1931). Works by Casas include those that decorated the famous artistic tavern of Els Quatre Gats. Some of Rusinyol's best works were executed during his first stay in Paris in 1889, particularly the two scenes set in the famous Montmartre Beer Garden of the Moulin de la Galette. Modernista sculpture is represented by Josep Llimona. There are decorative elements from buildings by the great Modernista trio, Domènech i Montaner, Puig i Cadafalch and Antoní Gaudí.

The second generation of Modernista artists is represented by Hermenegildo Anglada Camarasa, Josep Maria Sert, Ricard Canals, Joaquim Mir and Isidre Nonell.

The next section contains works by artists associated with **Noucentisme**, which represented both a return to classical models and a reaction against the stylistic eccentricities of Modernisme. Its main proponents included the sculptor Josep Clarà and the painter Joaquim Sunyer. Other key figures were the sculptor Manolo Hugué and the painter Xavier Nogués (1873-1941). There is a series of murals that Nogués painted for the Galerías Layetanas, a meeting place for Noucentista artists.

The last section displays works by some of the more avant-garde artists working in Catalunya in the second and third decades of the 20c, including Josep de Togores, Josep Mompou, Leando Cristòfol and Julio González. Particularly remarkable are the playful sculptures of Pau Gargallo. There is also a portrait of mesmerizing power by the young Salvador Dalí.

Parks and gardens of Montjuïc

Apart from the various museums and Olympic installations, Montjuïc is home to an incredible concentration of formal parks and gardens, the first of which was laid out in 1922. For the 1929 Exhibition Jean-Claude Nicolas Forestier was entrusted with remodelling the area. In recent years work has been undertaken to establish a number of new thematic gardens within the 250-hectare zone known as the Parc de Montjuïc. The parks are pleasant and safe enough during the day, although some zones are used for cruising, and occasional muggings are reported. At night, the deserted hillside becomes the haunt of drug-users and prostitutes; care should be exercised. The best way to enjoy Montjuïc's parks is to start at the top by taking the chair-lift to the fort and meandering down the hill on foot. Unless otherwise noted the gardens are open 10.00 to dusk and are free.

OPEN	**Jardí Botànic**: Mon-Sat 10.00-17.00, Sun & PH 10.00-15.00; June-Aug Mon-Sat 10.00-20.00 **Jardins de Joan Maragall**: Sat, Sun & PH 10.00-18.00 **Viver dels Tres Pins**: daily 8.00-19.00
LOCATION	**Jardí Botànic**: southern zone of Montjuïc, between the Castle and the Olympic stadium **Jardins de Joan Maragall**: the entrances are off Avinguda de l'Estadi and behind the MNAC **Jardins de Mossèn Cinto Verdaguer**: Avinguda Miramar **Jardins de Mossèn Costa i Llobera**: Carretera Miramar **Jardins del Teatre Grec**: off Passeig Santa Madrona and Avinguda Miramar **Mirador del Migdia**: off C/del Foc, C/Doctor Font i Quer and Passeig del Migdia **Viver dels Tres Pins**: Avinguda Miramar

JARDÍ BOTÀNIC This is the most recent addition to the park, featuring plants from around the world suitable for a Mediterranean climate, including species from China and Japan. Facilities include a snackbar and exhibition hall.

JARDINS DE JOAN MARAGALL This 3.6 hectare French-style formal garden, complete with fountains, topiary and a small lake, was laid out in 1970 by Joaquim Casamor as a complement to the Paulet Albeniz, a 1929 exhibition building used as a residence for visiting dignitaries.

JARDINS DE MOSSÈN CINTO VERDAGUER Joaquim Casamor designed this 4.3 hectare English-style garden in 1970 as a place of quiet contemplation, but also where a dramatic view over the city could be enjoyed. The space, once a quarry, is now equipped with fountains and faux waterfalls.

JARDINS DE MOSSÈN COSTA I LLOBERA The third of Casamor's gardens, this 6-hectare Mediterranean desert landscape descends the steep seaward slope of Montjuïc, from the castle to the port. The topography of the hill has created a micro-climate particularly suited to hot-weather plants: African, American and Australian species are represented, including spectacular cacti. This park is best accessed via the Barceloneta cablecar.

JARDINS DEL TEATRE GREC This compact garden was laid out by Forestier in 1922. Inspired by descriptions of the terraced gardens of ancient Babylon, the fountains evoke the Arabic-style gardens of the Generalife in Granada.

MIRADOR DEL MIGDIA Designed by Beth Galí, Jaume Benavent and Andreu Arriola, and inaugurated in 1992, this forest park is laid out along a series of switchbacks which descend the steep slopes below the fortress. The climate is temperate and vegetation typical of north-central Europe has been planted.

VIVER DELS TRES PINS Originally set up as the park's central nursery in the 1920s, a renovation and enlargement programme under the direction of Enric Batlle and Joan Roig was undertaken in 1985 and completed in 1993. Today it features a comprehensive collection of trees and plants which is dedicated to the German ecologist Petra Kelly, and which is used primarily for educational purposes.

CaixaForum

OPEN	Tues-Sun 10.00-20.00
CLOSED	Mon
CHARGES	Free admission
TELEPHONE	**934 768 600**
WWW.	**fundacio.lacaixa.es**
MAIN ENTRANCE	Avinguda Marquès de Comillas 6-8
DISABLED ACCESS	Full facilities
METRO/BUS	Espanya. Bus Turístic
SHOP	Good range of art books, designer souvenirs and accessories, including watches, jewellery and bags
EATING	Café serving snacks and meals

At least two temporary exhibitions run at any given time. There is an extensive programme of talks, films and concerts, as well as special activities for children. Video and media centre. Guided tours of the building.

Opened in 2002, CaixaForum is a contemporary art museum and cultural centre run by the foundation of La Caixa, Catalonia's largest building society. The foundation's important collections of Spanish and international art from the second half of the 20c was begun in 1985 and comprises around 800 works. It is installed in an important Modernista building and represents a laudable example of rehabilitation, but with its rather eccentric and inefficient layout it is not the best-suited space for an art museum.

THE BUILDING

The Modernista brick complex housing the museum is the Fabrica Casarramona, designed in 1911 by Puig i Cadafalch and awarded the city's 'best building' prize in 1913. Built at the end of the Modernista period in neo-Gothic style, its façade has been compared with Charles Barry's Houses of Parliament in London (1837-60). Originally a factory producing cotton thread and fabrics, the buildings were used as a police barracks until 1993. Mies van der Rohe's pavilion on the opposite side of the road provided the

CaixaForum

inspiration for Japanese architect Arata Isozaki, who designed the nearby Palau Sant Jordi Olympic stadium, to create a spectacular entrance to the new venue, comprising two steel trees that branch out to support a glass roof over a compact courtyard. One wall of the entrance space features a mural by American artist Sol Lewitt.

HIGHLIGHTS

Joseph Beuys, *Schmerzraum*

Juan Muñoz, *Waste Land* and *Conversation Piece* (*Hirshhorn*)

Miquel Navarro, *Des del terrat*

Cristina Iglesias, *Untitled M/m 1*

Ilya Kabakov, *For sale*

Jannis Kounellis, *Untitled*

Richard Long, *Catalan Circle*

Allan McCollum, *Plaster Surrogates*

The collection is exhibited on a rotational basis in three large spaces, with displays changing every few months. However, some of the installations are on permanent display.

The holdings are divided into two collections: Spanish Art 1947-79, and Contemporary Art from 1980.

SPANISH ART 1947-79

The earliest works are by the Dau al Set collective, which played an important role in the development of art in Catalunya. Members included Modest Cuixart and Antoni Tàpies. This is followed by artists whose work spans several decades, including members of the El Paso group, such as Antonio Saura, Luis Feito and Maneul Millares. Eduardo Chillida and Pablo Palazuelo are also well represented. Artists active in the the 1960s include sculptor Jorge Oteiza and painters Lucio Muñoz, José Guerrero, Josep Guinovert and Manuel Mompó. There are important figurative works by Eduardo Arroyo and Equipo Crónica. The 1970s are represented by Joan Hernández Pijuan, Ignacio Tovar and Patricio Vélez.

CONTEMPORARY ART FROM 1980

This collection begins with work produced in the 1980s by Spanish and international artists who were active in previous decades, including Joseph Beuys, Antoni Tàpies, Jannis Kounnellis, Donald Judd, Carl Andre and Mario Merz. Artists who were emerging in the 1980s include Ferran García Sevilla, Juan Navarro Baldeweg, José Manuel Broto, Miquel Barceló, Perejaume, Julian Schnabel, Gerhard Richter and Sigmar Polke.

Schmerzraum (1983), or Sick Room, by Joseph Beuys, consists of a lead-lined space accessed by a glass door and empty except for a bare light bulb, two suspended rings and a telephone. Beuys was one of the most influential artists of the second half of the 20c. A reluctant pilot for Germany during World War II, he completed his art studies in Düsseldorf in 1952.

The new wave of British sculptors at the beginning of the 1980s is well represented with works by Anish Kapoor, Julian Opie, Tony Cragg and Richard Deacon. Spanish sculptors from the same period include Miquel Navarro, Eva Lootz, Juan Muñoz, Cristina Iglesias, Susana Solano, Txomin Badiola and Francisco Leiro. American artists incude Haim Steinbach, Cindy Sherman, Bill Viola and Tim Rollins.

Des del terrat (*From the floor*; 1985-6), a collection of terracotta and glass-based structures, is part of Miquel Navarro's architectural series *The City*, which he describes as a sculptural landscape. The artist draws on the rich and romantic Iberian past and his home town of Mislata, Valencia, for inspiration.

Alan McCollum, a sculptor from Los Angeles, made his mark in the 1980s with works that seek to challenge our concept of art and its role in the world of consumer culture. His 'Surrogates' are meant to be false pieces of art which ask us to consider whether substitute art, which is not actually art, can fulfil art's function.

Russian-born Ilya Kabakoz has become known for his dramatic

constructions such as *For Sale* (1993), an example of his 'total installations', designed to overwhelm and draw the viewer in to the atmosphere created by the work.

Juan Muñoz developed as a sculptor in late 1970s London. In *Conversation Piece* (*Hirshorn*; 1995), one of several works on this theme, life-sized semi-abstract figures are locked in an animated discussion; or are two threatening the third?

From the 1990s there is work by Rachel Whiteread, Mike Kelley, Fiona Rae, Sam Taylor-Wood, Tacita Dean and Juan Uslé.

Joan Miró Foundation

OPEN	Tues-Sat: Oct-June 10.00-19.00, July-Sept 10.00-20.00; Thur until 21.30; Sun and PH 10.00-14.30
CLOSED	Mon; 1/1, 6/1, Good Friday and 25/12
CHARGES	€7.20 for all exhibitions; €3.90 senior citizens and students; €3.60 for temporary exhibitions only; €1.80 for senior citizens and students. Free with Articket; Discount with Bus Turístic and Barcelona Card. Price includes audioguide
TELEPHONE	**934 439 470**
WWW.	**bcn.fjmiro.es**
MAIN ENTRANCE	Parc de Montjuïc
DISABLED ACCESS	Fully accessible for wheelchair users, with wheelchairs available
METRO/BUS STOP	Espanya + Bus 50 or Paral.lel + Funicular de Montjuïc. Bus Turístic
SHOP	Gift shop with extensive range of Miró-themed ceramics, accessories, posters, prints, stationery, toys and jewellery. Bookshop with good stock of magazines and books on Miró, other artists, design, architecture and Barcelona
EATING	Café in courtyard serves snacks. Restaurant has international menu

There is always at least one temporary exhibition, often featuring major international artists, and a programme of cultural events that includes concerts and children's activities. Guided tours at 12.30 Sat and Sun.

The Fundació Joan Miró was built in 1972-4 to house a large group of works donated by Joan Miró. The displays include paintings, sculptures, drawings, tapestries and graphic work. As well as the works donated by Miró himself, the Foundation also holds the collection of his wife, Pilar Juncosa, and a range of works by leading 20c artists.

Joan Miró was born in 1893 in Barcelona and spent much of his life in the city, as well as long periods in Paris and Palma in Mallorca, where he died in 1983. He is buried in Montjuïc cemetery, near the Foundation.

Joan Miró Foundation

THE BUILDING

The museum is one of only two buildings executed in Barcelona after the Civil War by the outstanding locally-born architect Josep Lluís Sert, a close friend of Miró's who had previously designed the artist's studio in Mallorca. The Foundation is set within the luxuriant shrubbery of the Montjuïc Park, and centred around a patio commanding magnificent views over Barcelona. Sculptures by Miró adorn the terraces, and the building and its grounds also incorporate works by other artists, most notably garden sculptures by Calder and Chillida. The building was substantially extended in 1987-8 and 2001 by Jaume Freixa, who had worked with Sert on the original scheme.

HIGHLIGHTS

Tapestry of the Foundation and *Mercury Fountain*	Room 11
Female Nude and *Portrait of a Young Girl*	Room 16
Morning Star (1940) and *Morning Star* (1946)	Room 17

The permanent collection is located on the ground and first floors, plus three rooms in the basement. Temporary exhibitions are held on the ground floor in Rooms 1-10.

GROUND FLOOR

To access the displays you cross a courtyard with a view across Barcelona and turn right into the first room.

ROOMS 11-12 The large *Tapestry of the Foundation* (1979) was designed for the Foundation. It is one of Miró's *sobreteixims*, a textile combining elements of painting, collage and tapestry. As you walk up a short ramp to access Room 12, outside on your left is the *Mercury Fountain* by Alexander Calder which was built for the Spanish Republican Government's Pavilion at the Paris World Fair in 1937, where it was displayed in front of Picasso's *Guernica*. The fountain commemorates the mercury mining town of Almadén, which suffered severe damage in the Civil War. Room 12 is dominated by two brightly-coloured synthetic resin sculptures, *Lovers playing with Almond Blossom*, which were a model for a sculptural group at La Defense, Paris, in 1975. The room also contains bronze works dating from 1968-75, revealing the artist's

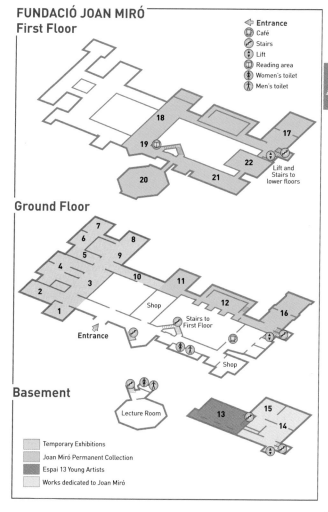

FUNDACIÓ JOAN MIRÓ

First Floor

- ⬳ Entrance
- ☕ Café
- 🚶 Stairs
- 🛗 Lift
- 📖 Reading area
- 🚺 Women's toilet
- 🚹 Men's toilet

18

19

17

22

Lift and Stairs to lower floors

20   21

Ground Floor

7
6   8
5   9
4
3   10   11
2   12
1   16

Shop

Stairs to First Floor

Entrance

Shop

Basement

Lecture Room

13   15

14

Temporary Exhibitions

Joan Miró Permanent Collection

Espai 13 Young Artists

Works dedicated to Joan Miró

147

inventiveness and sense of humour, including *Sunbird* (1946),
Moon Bird (1946-9), *The Bird makes its Nest in the Fingers in Flower*
(1969) and *Figure* (1969).

BASEMENT

Steps lead down to Espai 13, which displays work by young artists
and is sometimes used for temporary exhibitions.

ROOMS 14-15 Accessed by a separate staircase, these rooms
contain a collection of contemporary art in homage to Joan Miró.
Donated by friends and admirers, these include pieces by Léger,
Motherwell, Ernst, Saura, Rauschenberg, Moore, Duchamp,
Millares, Penrose, Brossa and Chillida. There are also
photographic portraits by Man Ray, Arnold Newman and Francesc
Català-Roca.

GROUND FLOOR

ROOM 16 Go back upstairs to reach this large space, also known
as the Sala Joan Prats, which is divided into two parts and
contains biographical information about his early life and career.
On the right as you enter is *Peacock*, a drawing executed when he
was just 14 and a pupil at Barcelona's Llotja art school. *Mas d'en
Poca* (1914) is one of his first catalogued paintings. *Female nude*
(1917), a drawing from the Joan Prats collection, is one of his
finest early works. *Chapel of Sant Joan d'Horta* (1917) shows how
he was influenced by Fauvism, a style he had clearly abandoned
when he painted *Portrait of a Young Girl* (1918). This idealized
portrait in oil on paper, reflects the two sources of Modernista
inspiration, the medieval and oriental. The second half of the room
shows how Miró's style developed very quickly after he returned to
Paris in 1924, becoming abstract and poetic, as illustrated by *The
Wine Bottle* (1924), *Painting (the white glove)* (1925), *The Music-hall
Usher* (1925) and *Untitled (Tree in the Wind)* (1929).

FIRST FLOOR

ROOM 17 From the 1930s, Miró started to experiment with collage, represented by *Preliminary Collage for Painting* (1933), which shows his skill at balancing colour, forms and textures. Also in this section is the brutal work *Head* (1937) and *Painting on Masonite* (1936), which is part of a series expressing his outrage at the Civil War.

Morning Star (1940), a frenetic work in tempera on paper, is an expression of the artist's dismay and horror at the outbreak of World War II. It is one in a series of 23 paintings referred to as the *Constellations* and was donated by his wife, after whom this section of the room is named, the Sala Pilar Juncosa. The themes used in the *Constellations* recurred in his work from then on, as shown by *Woman Dreaming of Escape* (1945), *Woman and Bird in the Night* (1945) and *Morning Star* (1946). The room contains other donations from Pilar Juncosa, including *Man and Woman in Front of a Pile of Excrement* (1935).

ROOM 18-19 Turn right down the ramp and walk to the other end, which contains large-format works executed after Josep Lluís Sert had built him a huge studio at his house just outside Palma in Mallorca. Paintings include *Woman with Three Hairs, Birds and Constellations* (1973), *The Gold of the Azur* (1967), *Poem III* (1968) and *Catalan Peasant in the Moonlight* (1968). *Sunbird* (1968), in Carrara marble, is a larger version of the earlier bronze sculpture in Room 12.

From here you can go out onto the terrace, which features a variety of sculptures and offers fantastic views across the city.

ROOM 20 An octagonal tower space contains three triptychs: the grey canvases of *The Hope of the Man Condemned to Death, 1,2,3* (1974), *Painting on a White Background for the Cell of a Man in a Solitary Confinement 1,2,3* and the brightly-coloured *Fireworks 1,2,3* (1974).

ROOM 21 This corridor area displays bronze sculpture including *Head and Bird* (1966) and *Woman* (1970).

SALA K This final section opened in 2001 and contains 23 works on long-term loan from the Japanese collector Kazumasa Katsuta, as well as one painting from his family. The works span his career from 1914-73, and include *Untitled (Seated Nude)* (1916); *Woman, bird, stars* (1942); *The Red of the Swallows and the Iridescent Pink* (1947) and *A Break in the Sky gives us Hope* (1954). The vibrant large-format works in the second part of the room include *The Lark's Wing ringed in the Blue of Gold meets the Heart of the Poppy asleep on the Field adorned with Diamonds* (1967) and the orange *Drop of Water on Pink Snow* (1968).

on route

Estadi Olímpic, Av. Marquès de Comillas. Magnificent eclectic structure built by Pere Domènech i Roura for the sports events of the International Exhibition of 1929. Now the home ground of Espanyol, one of Barcelona's two football clubs. **M** Espanya. Bus Turístic

Font Màgica, Av. de la Reina Maria Cristina. This elaborate fountain at the foot of Montjuïc, below the MNAC, springs to life with a colourful spot-light hydraulic display (Thur-Sun 20.00-24.00; at 22.30 a musical accompaniment adds to the extravaganza). Kitsch but beautiful.

Fundació Fran Daurel, Poble Espanyol (Porta del Carme), Av. Marquès de Comillas. Daily 10.00-19.00; *T* 934 234 172. Contemporary art collections of the Catalan industrialist Fran Daurel. Includes paintings by Antoni Tàpies, Miquel Barceló and José Maria Sicilia, drawings by Dalí, ceramics by Picasso and graphic work by Miró and Chillida. Only accessible with Poble Espanyol admission. **M** Espanya. Bus Turístic

Galeria Olímpica, Av. Marquès de Comillas. Mon-Fri; Oct-March 10.00-13.00, 16.00-18.00; April-Sept 10.00-14.00, 16.00-19.00; *T* 934 260 660. Behind the stadium, this museum contains exhibits related to the 1992 Olympic and Paralympic Games. **M** Espanya. Bus Turístic

Estadi Olímpic

Mies van der Rohe Pavilion, Av. Marquès de Comillas. Daily 10.00-20.00; *T* 934 234 016, www.miesbcn.es. Reconstruction in original location of Mies van der Rohe's marble and glass structure German Pavilion (Pavelló d'Alemanya) for the International Exhibition of 1929. *M* Espanya. Bus Turístic

Museu d'Arqueologia de Catalunya, Passeig de Santa Madrona. Tues-Sat 9.30-19.00, Sun and PH 10.00-14.30; closed Mon; *T* 934 246 577. Roman mosaics, finds from the Greek settlement at Empúries, and a superb room devoted to Carthaginian finds from Ibiza, among which is the celebrated *Dama de Ibiza*. Temporary exhibitions. Book and gift shop. *M* Espanya

Museu de les Arts Escèniques, Plaça de Margarida Xirgu, near the Museu d'Arqueologia. Tues-Sat 10.00-13.00, 17.00-19.30, Sun 10.00-14.00; closed Mon; *T* 932 273 916. Museum of the Performing Arts with permanent and temporary exhibitions charting the history and development of theatre and performance. Bookshop. *M* Poble Sec, Espanya

Museu Etnològic, Passeig de Santa Madrona. Tues-Sun 10.00-19.00; closed Mon; *T* 934 246 807. Art and crafts from Spain, South America, Africa and Asia. Temporary exhibitions. *M* Espanya

Museu Militar, Castell de Montjuïc. Daily: mid March-Oct 9.30-20.00; Nov-mid March 9.30-17.00; *T* 933 298 613. Weapons, helmets, uniforms, model soldiers and paintings. Archaeological exhibits found on Montjuïc are displayed on the upper floor. Temporary exhibitions. Shop and café. *M* Paral.lel and funicular

Plaça d'Espanya Looking towards Montjuïc

Palau Sant Jordi, Av. Marquès de Comillas. The elegant covered Olympix structure was built in 1985-90 by the Japanese architect Arata Isozaki. The sculptural installation in front of the building was created by Aiko Miyawaki, Isozaki's wife. *M* Espanya. Bus Turístic

Poble Espanyol, Av. Marquès de Comillas. Mon 9.00-20.00, Tues-Thur 9.00-2.00, Fri & Sat 9.00-4.00, Sun 9.00-24.00; *T* 933 257 866, www.poble-espanyol.com. Built for the International Exhibition in 1929, the complex comprises surprisingly authentic reproductions of buildings from all over Spain. Shops, cafés and restaurants. *M* Espanya. Bus Turístic

Torre de Calatrava, Av. Marquès de Comillas. This graceful steel structure, painted white, was designed by Santiago Calatrava and is a telecommunications ariel. *M* Espanya. Bus Turístic

eating and drinking

AT THE MUSEUMS
€ **CaixaForum**, *T* 934 768 669. Vast, well-designed café serving snacks and full meals. Excellent fixed-price lunch menu, with dishes such as baked monkfish with tomato-flavoured olive oil

and white chocolate mousse. Popular with arty crowd.

Fundació Joan Miró, *T* 933 290 768. The café has tables in a lovely courtyard, but snacks are limited to just a few sandwiches and cakes. The restaurant section has magnificent views across the city and a menu includes Italian, Indian and Greek dishes, as well as Catalan specialities, all served on white plates decorated with Miró motifs.

Museu Nacional d'Art de Catalunya, *T* 936 220 376. A new café, serving drinks, snacks and full meals, is being installed as part of the renovations.

SURROUNDING AREA

€ **Bar Primavera**, C/Nou de la Rambla 192, *T* 933 293 062. If you walk down the hill after visiting the Miró Foundation, stop off at this pretty outdoor café near the funicular track. *M* Paral.lel

El Sortidor, Placa Sortidor 5, *T* 934 418 518. Homemade pasta and other great Italian dishes. In business since 1908 and run by family from Turin. *M* Paral.lel, Poble Sec

Kasbah, C/Vilai Vilà 82, *T* 933 298 384. North African, Middle Eastern and French dishes. Good tagines and couscous. *M* Paral.lel

La Bella Napoli, C/Margarit 14, *T* 934 425 056. Cosy Italian-run restaurant with tasty pasta and pizzas, baked in a wood oven. *M* Poble Sec

Quimet y Quimet, C/Poeta Cabanyes 25, *T* 934 423 142. Classic tapas bar which is worth seeking out. Family run and open for a 100 years, the only drawback is the lack of space. Good wines, vermouths and beers. *M* Paral.lel

Sirvent, C/Parlament 56, *T* 934 412 720. Open for 60 years, fabulous bar for ice cream, *horchata* and *turrón* nougat. Family-run, from Xixona in Alicante. Open only from April to Christmas. *M* Poble Sec

Tivoli's Bistro, C/Magallenes 35, *T* 933 314 017, www.tivolisbistro.com. Excellent Thai food, with good value taster menu. *M* Palal.lel

€€ **El Abrevadero**, C/Vila i Vilá 77, *T* 934 413 893. Upmarket restaurant serving superior creative Catalan cuisine. Taster menu. Good value set lunch. Seasonal menu. *M* Paral.lel

Cuixart, C/Vila i Vilà 53, *T* 934 413 078. Imaginative menu with international influences. Tables in pretty garden. Run by Laura

Cuixart, the daughter of the renowned artist Modest Cuixart.
M Paral.lel

Elche, C/Vila i Vilà 71, *T* 934 413 089. Non-touristy paella specialist popular with locals. *M* Paral.lel

Lliure, El Restaurante del Teatre, Passeig Santa Madrona 40-46, *T* 933 250 075. Designer restaurant in new theatre in former Palau de l'Agricultura. Mediterranean-Catalan cuisine created by renowned chef Sergi Blasi. *M* Poble Sec

Mesón Morriña, C/Parlament 46, *T* 934 419 336. Very popular family-run place that uses top-quality ingredients and also has terrific wines. *M* Poble Sec

€€€ **Rías de Galicia**, C/Lleida 7, *T* 934 248 152. Upmarket Galician seafood restaurant, five minutes' walk from the MNAC. First-class lobster, oysters and langoustines. *M* Espanya, Poble Sec

BARS & CLUBS

Barcelona Rouge, C/Poeta Cabanyes 21, *T* 934 424 985. Daily 23.00-3.00. Cocktail lounge with carpets, walls and furniture in different shades of red. DJs at weekends. *M* Paral.lel

La Terrazza, Poble Espanyol, Av. Marquès de Comillas, *T* 932 724 980. Thur-Sat 24.00-6.00. Very popular open-air club specializing in garage music. In winter it transfers to adjacent indoor space, Discothèque. *M* Espanya

Los Juanele, C/Aldana 4. Thur, Fri and Sat from 22.00. Non-touristy flamenco club popular with Andalusians. *M* Paral.lel

Nitsa Club, Sala Apolo, C/Nou de la Rambla 113, *T* 933 010 090, www.nitsa.com. Fri and Sat 1.00-6.00. Three spaces playing pop, house and drum and bass. Very busy. *M* Paral.lel

Tinta Roja, C/Creu dels Molers 17, *T* 934 433 243. Atmospheric bar, run by a couple of Argentinian tango dancers. Live music, dancing and Argentinian drinks. *M* Poble Sec

Vip Club, Poble Espanyol, Av. Marqus de Comillas, *T* 934 249 309. Fri and Sat 24.00-7.00. Club with various spaces designed by Mariscal inside the Torres de Avila, the towers which form the entrance to the Poble Espanyol. *M* Espanya

entertainment

**INFORMATION
TICKETS
CINEMA
THEATRE, OPERA, DANCE
MUSIC
CLUBS**

INFORMATION

The *Guía del Ocio* (www.guiadelociobcn.es) listings magazine comes out every Thursday and covers cinema, theatre, concerts, exhibitions, restaurants and nightlife. The daily papers contain entertainment information and on Fridays publish entertainment supplements. Look out for *Metropolitan*, a free monthly English magazine available in hotels and some bars and boutiques. The monthly leaflets *Teatre BCN*, *Barcelona Cultural Activities* and *Informatiu Musical* are available from tourist offices and the information centres at the Palau de la Virreina (La Rambla 99) and the Centre d'Art Santa Mònica (La Rambla 7).

TICKETS

As well as from the respective box offices, concert, opera and theatre tickets are available from **Tel-Entrada** (*T* 902 101 212, www.telentrada.com) and **ServiCaixa** (*T* 902 332 211, www.serviticket.com). Tickets can also be purchased from the ServiCaixa machines at branches of La Caixa bank, although foreign credit cards may not work.

FNAC, Triangle Centre, Plaça de Catalunya, *T* 933 441 800. Tickets for pop concerts and other events

El Corte Inglés, Plaça de Catalunya and branches, *T* 902 400 222

CINEMA

The cinemas listed below offer foreign films in VO (version original), subtitled in Spanish or Catalan.

Casablanca, Passeig de Gràcia 115, *T* 932 184 345. Small multi-screen cinema showing first-run films. *M* Diagonal

Filmoteca, Av. de Sarrià 33, *T* 934 107 590. The Catalan government film venue; regular retrospective screenings. *M* Hospital Clinic

Icaria-Yelmo, C/de Salvador Espriu 61, *T* 932 217 585. Comfortable multiplex at the Villa Olímpica by the beach; new films. *M* Ciutadella

Maldá, C/Pi 5, T 933 178 529. The Old City's repertory cinema. *M* Liceu

Méliès, C/Villaroel, *T* 934 510 051. Repertory house specializing in oldies. *M* Urgell

Renoir Floridblanca, C/Floridablanca 135, *T* 934 263 337. Seven-room cineplex; second-run foreign films. *M* Universitat, Sant Antoni

Renoir-Les Corts, C/Eugeni d'Ors 12, *T* 934 905 510. Six-screen repertory cinema. *M* Les Corts

Verdi & Verdi Park, C/Verdi 32 and C/Torrijos 49, *T* 932 370 516. Nine screens. Recent releases in VO, although recently European films are favoured over English-language productions. *M* Fontana

THEATRE, OPERA, DANCE

Gran Teatre del Liceu, La Rambla 51-59, *T* 934 859 913, www.liceubarcelona.com. Barcelona's prestigious opera house: soloists and theatrical productions. *M* Liceu

Guasch Teatre, C/Aragó 140, *T* 934 513 462, www.guaschteatre.com. Mid-sized venue for Spanish and Catalan language theatre. *M* Urgell

Institut del Teatre, Plaça Margarida Xirgu, *T* 932 273 900, www.diba.es/iteatre. Barcelona's theatre institute has two venues for productions directed by its faculty and students, mostly in Catalan. *M* Poble Sec, Espanya. *Bus* 55

L'Espai,Travessera de Gràcia 63, *T* 934 143 133, http://cultura.gencat.net/espai. Dance and music venue. Spanish and Catalan artists, avant-garde to flamenco. *FGC* Gràcia

Mercat de les Flors, Plaça Margarida Xirgu, C/Lleida 59, *T* 934 261 875, www.bcn.es/mercatflors. A spacious new multi-venue in the old flower market, hosting an eclectic programme of music, dance and theatre. *M* Poble Sec, Espanya. *Bus* 55

Teatre Lliure, Plaça Margarida Xirgu, *T* 932 892 770, www.teatrelliure.com. Contemporary dance, theatre and spoken-word in Castilian, Catalan and English. *M* Poble Sec, Espanya. *Bus* 55

Teatre Nacional de Catalunya, Plaça de les Arts 1, *T* 933 065 700, www.tnc.es. Varied theatre from classical to contemporary, performed in Catalan. *M* Glòries, Marina

Teatre Poliorama, La Rambla 115, *T* 933 188 181, www.teatrepoliorama.com. Set in a Modernista building on the Ramblas, lively kinetic theatre featuring local troupes such as Tricycle. *M* Catalunya

Teatre Romea, C/Hospital 51, *T* 93 301 4750, www.fundacioromea.org. Conterts and plays in Catalan and Castilian. *M* Liceu

MUSIC

CLASSICAL

L'Auditori, C/Lepant 150, *T* 932 479 300, English speakers *T* 933 262 946, www.auditori.com. Mammoth orchestral venue. *M* Glòries, Marina

Palau de la Música Catalana, C/Sant Francesc de Paula 2, *T* 932 957 200, www.palaumusica.org. Domènech i Monaner's magnificent Modernista concert hall (p 71). A wide choice of concerts from classical and choral to popular. *M* Urquinaona

Auditori Winterthur, L'ILLA shopping centre, Diagonal 547, *T* 932 901 090. Another large venue, mostly classical music. *M* María Cristina

La Casa Elizalde, C/València 302, *T* 934 880 590, www.casaelizalde.com. *M* Passeig de Gràcia

FLAMENCO

Los Juanele, C/Aldana 4, no phone. A grungy but genuine *tabla* for true flamenco fans. *M* Paral.lel

Los Tarantos, Plaça Reial 17, *T* 933 183 067, www.masimas.com. The most touristy of Barcelona's flamenco offerings; a formal crowd-pleasing show. *M* Liceu

Soniquete, C/Milans 5, no phone. Barcelona's newest *tabla*, a tiny and smoky room a short walk from Plaça Reial. *M* Jaume I

JAZZ

Harlem Jazz Club, C/Comtessa de Sobradiel 8, *T* 933 100 755. Old City institution: jazz and contemporary in cramped quarters. *M* Liceu

Jamboree, Plaça Reial 17, *T* 933 017 564. Expensive jazz and blues in the Plaça Reial, most concerts start at 23.00. *M* Liceu

Jazz Sí Club, C/Requesens 2, *T* 933 290 020. Semi-formal evening jams are the speciality of this popular venue. *M* Sant Antoni

La Boite, Av. Diagonal 477, **T** 933 191 789, www.masimas.com. Nightclub with varied music, blues to popular. **M** Hospital Clínic

La Cova del Drac, C/Vallmajor 33, **T** 933 191 789, www.masimas.com. Another respected city jazz venue. Spanish and international groups. **FGC** Muntaner

ROCK AND POP

Bikini, C/Deu i Mata 105, **T** 933 220 800, www.bikinibcn.com. One of Barcelona's oldest and most venerated rock clubs. Top national and international groups. **M** Les Corts

Luz de Gas, C/Muntaner 246, **T** 932 097 711, www.luzdegas.com. Rock, blues and jazz in fairly chic surroundings. **M** Hospital Clínic

Nitsa Club, Sala Apolo, C/Nou de la Rambla 113, **T** 933 010 090, www.sala-apolo.com. Long-standing jazz and rock club. **M** Paral.lel

Razzmatazz, C/Almògavers 122, **T** 933 208 200, www.salarazzmatazz.com. Along with sister-clubs Razzmatazz 2 and 3, all part of the same complex, this club specializes in garage, punk, metal and progressive groups. **M** Marina, Bogatella

CLUBS

Agua de Luna, C/Viladomat 211, **T** 934 100 440, www.aguadeluna.com. Latin music, particularly salsa and merengue. **M** Urgell

Club Danzatoria, Av. Trias Fargas, Marina Village, **T** 932 687 430, www.clubdanzatoria.com. Several rooms at this beachside house and techno club. **M** Ciutadella Vila Olímpica

Discothèque, Av. Marquès de Comillas, **T** 932 724 980, www.nightsungroup.com. House and R&B. **M** Espanya

Distrito Diagonal, Av. Diagonal 442, **T** 934 154 635, www.distritodiagonal.com. House and fusion music. **M** Diagonal

Universal, C/Marià Cubi 182, **T** 932 013 596. House and pop music. **FGC** Muntaner

planning

**TOURIST OFFICES
GETTING THERE
GETTING AROUND
MUSEUM PASSES
OTHER ESSENTIALS
PLACES TO STAY
ART CALENDAR**

TOURIST OFFICES

The **Spanish National Tourist Office** provides an extensive range of maps and leaflets on accommodation, culture, transport, sport and festivals.

IN THE UK

Spanish National Tourist Office, 22-23 Manchester Square, London W1U 3PX, *T* 020 7486 8077, *F* 020 7486 8034, brochure line *T* 09063 640 630, www.spain.info, info.londres@tourspain.es

Tourist Office of Catalunya, 17 Fleet Street, 3rd Floor, London EC4Y 1AA, *T* 020 7583 8855, *F* 020 7583 8877, www.gencat.es/turisme

IN THE USA AND CANADA

New York: **Tourist Office of Spain**, 666 5th Avenue, 35th floor, New York, NY 10103, *T* 1 212 265 8822, *F* 1 212 265 8864, www.okspain.org, oetny@tourspain.es

Los Angeles: **Tourist Office of Spain**, 8383 Wilshire Boulevard, Suite 956, Beverly Hills, CA 90211, *T* 1 323 658 7188, *F* 1 323 658 1061, losangeles@tourspain.es

Chicago: **Tourist Office of Spain**, Water Tower Place, Suite 915 East, 845 North Michigan Ave, Chicago, Ill 60611, *T* 1 312 642 1992, *F* 1 312 642 9817, chicago@tourspain.es

Miami: **Tourist Office of Spain**, 1221 Brickell Ave, Suite 1850, Miami, *T* 1 305 358 1992, *F* 1 305 358 8223, oetmiami@tourspain.es

Canada: **Tourist Office of Spain**, 2 Bloor St West, Suite 3402, Toronto, Ontario M4W 3E2, *T* 1 416 961 3131, *F* 1 416 961 1992, www.tourspain.toronto.on.ca, toronto@tourspain.es

IN BARCELONA
Turisme de Barcelona, *T* 906 301 282 from Spain, *T* 933 689 730 from abroad, www.barcelonaturisme.com

Main office: Plaça de Catalunya 17 (Corte Inglés side): Mon-Sun 9.00-21.00. Information, hotel reservation service and book and gift shop.

Branches: Town Hall, Plaça de Sant Jaume: Mon-Fri 9.00-20.00, Sat 10.00-20.00, Sun and PH 10.00-14.00. Sants train station: June-Sept, Mon-Sun 8.00-20.00; Oct-May, Mon-Fri 8.00-20.00, Sat, Sun and PH 8.00-14.00. Airport, Terminals A and B: Mon-Sun 9.00-21.00.

There are also information kiosks at key points around the city, including the Sagrada Família, and multilingual staff in red jackets walk the streets.

Turisme de Catalunya, *T* 932 384 000, www.gencat.es/turisme, Palau Robert, Passeig de Gràcia 107. Mon-Sat 10.00-19.00, Sun 10.00-14.00. Information on Catalunya, as well as a book and gift shop.

There are also culture and tourism information centres at the Palau de la Virreina (La Rambla 99, *T* 933 017 775) and the Centre d'Art Santa Mònica (La Rambla 7, *T* 933 162 810).

General information is available on the municipal helpline *T* 010, or *T* 934 027 000 from outside Barcelona. The city council website, www.bcn.es, provides general and cultural information in English.

GETTING THERE
BY AIR
El Prat International Airport is 12km (7.5 miles) south of the city centre. Iberia, British Airways and Air Europa use Terminal B; easyJet and bmibaby, Terminal A. The Barcelona-Madrid shuttle (Pont Aeri/Puente Aereo) uses C, *T* 932 983 838, www.aena.es.

FROM THE UK
bmibaby, *T* 0870 264 2229, www.bmibaby.com. Departures from East Midlands and Manchester

British Airways, *T* 0870 850 9850, www.ba.com. Departures from London Heathrow, Manchester and Birmingham

easyJet, *T* 0871 7500 100, www.easyjet.com. Departures from London Gatwick, Luton and Liverpool

Iberia, *T* 0845 601 2854, www.iberia.com. Departures from London Heathrow and Manchester

FROM IRELAND
Iberia, *T* 1 407 3017, www.iberia.com. Departures from Dublin

FROM THE USA AND CANADA
Air Canda, *T* 1 888 247 2262, www.aircanada.ca

Iberia, *T* 1 800 772 4642, www.iberia.com. Departures from Los Angeles. From New York and Chicago via Madrid. From Miami with one stop

Delta Airlines, *T* 1 800 241 4141, www.delta.com. Departures from New York and Atlanta

Lufthansa, *T* 1 800 399-LUFT, www.lufthansa-usa.com. Departures from New York and other cities via Frankfurt

FROM AUSTRALIA
Air France, *T* 02 9244 2100, www.airfrance.com/au. Departures from Sydney, Melbourne, Auckland, Brisbane and Perth via Paris

Lauda Air, *T* 02 9251 6155, www.lauda-air.com. Departures from Sydney via Kuala Lumpur

Olympic Airways, *T* 02 9251 2044, www.olympic-airways.com. Departures from Sydney and Melbourne via Athens

IN BARCELONA
Iberia has offices at C/Diputació 258, *T* 93 401 3355, and Plaça d'Espanya, *T* 93 325 7358

BY TRAIN
Using **Eurostar** from Waterloo International Terminal in London to Paris, the journey to Barcelona takes a total of around 18 hours. Information from Eurostar, *T* 0870 518 6186, www.eurostar.com. Or contact **Rail Europe**, *T* 0870 584 8848, www.raileurope.co.uk), or visit the **Rail Europe Travel Shop** at 179 Piccadilly, London W1V 0BA.

BY COACH
Eurolines runs a regular service from London to Barcelona. Coaches leave from Victoria Coach Station and the journey time is about 25 hours. Information *T* 0870 514 3219, www.eurolines.co.uk.

GETTING TO THE CITY CENTRE FROM THE AIRPORT
The **Aerobus** service runs to Plaça de Catalunya every 12 minutes

from 6.00–24.00. Fare approx. €3.50.

Trains leave the airport every 30 minutes from approx. 6.00-22.30 and stop at Sants (the main rail station), Plaça de Catalunya and Arc de Triomf. Fare approx. €2.5.

A metro line is under construction. A taxi to the centre costs €15-€20 including supplements.

GETTING AROUND

Public transport in Barcelona is cheap and efficient. Tickets are all flat-fare and there is a wealth of money-saving multi-trip tickets. **TMB**, the public transport company, has information centres at Universitat, Diagonal, Sagrada Família and Sants metro stations, and also at the FGC local train stations at Plaça de Catalunya, Plaça de Espanya and Provença. Call *T* 934 120 000 or the municipal helpline *T* 010 for information. Comprehensive information in English is available on the website, www.tmb.net. For information on facilities for disabled travellers, call *T* 934 860 752. Metro maps are available at the ticket booths at all stations and bus maps are available from tourist offices.

TRAVEL PASSES AND TICKETS

A single ticket for the bus or metro costs €1.05. The basic travelcard, or *targeta*, is the **T-10**, which costs €5.80 and allows ten rides on the metro, bus, FGC trains and Renfe local trains (*rodalies*) within Zone (*Corona*) 1, which covers just about everywhere you are likely to want to go in the city. Cards must be stamped in a machine at the front of buses, or put through the turnstile for the metro and trains. The card may be shared by two or more people, provided it is stamped the appropriate number of times per journey. Changes as part of a journey are allowed within 75 minutes, but you must reinsert your ticket in the stamping machine (it will not be stamped twice).

The **T-Dia** is a one-day travelcard covering unlimited travel and costs €5. Travelcards, called *abonaments*, are also available for €8 for two days, €11.30 for three days, €14.50 for four days and €17.30 for five days.

All the above are available at metro and FGC stations. Travelcards are also sold at some newsstands and lottery shops. You can also get them from ServiCaixa machines (payable by credit card), which are found in major branches of La Caixa bank, usually next to the cash machine.

The **Barcelona Card** allows unlimited travel for 24, 48 or 72 hours, as well as discounts on museum entrances, city sights, entertainment and in some shops and restaurants. It costs approx. €17, €20 and €23 respectively and is available from municipal tourist offices.

BY METRO

Trains run 5.00-24.00 Mon-Thur and Sun; 5.00-2.00 Fri, Sat and eves before PH. Most of the metro system is currently not easy for people with physical disabilities or in wheelchairs to use. Line 2 is the exception, with lifts and ramps at all stations, and there are lifts at some stations on Line 1. It is generally safe but beware of pickpockets.

BY BUS

Routes and the direction the bus is going are marked on all stops, making them very easy to use. Buses start at 5.00 or 6.00 and run until 22.30-24.00, depending on the route. You can buy a single flatfare ticket from the driver (change given) or stamp your travelcard in the machine at the front of the bus. Always get on at the front and off in the middle. Buses are single decker with low boarding platforms and an increasing number have electronic ramps and a designated space for wheelchair users. Night buses run from 22.30 to about 5.00. Most routes cross Plaça de Catalunya and all are equipped for wheelchairs.

The **TombBus** is a luxury service for shoppers that runs from Plaça de Catalunya up Passeig de Gràcia and along Diagonal. A single ticket costs about €1.40.

For details of the **Tourist Bus** (Bus Turístic), which is also an excellent way of getting around, see p 168.

BY FGC TRAIN

The Ferrocarrils de la Generalitat de Catalunya is a commuter train network which runs underground through the city centre just like the metro and has terminals in Plaça d'Espanya and Plaça de Catalunya. They serve not only such nearby districts as Gràcia and Sarrià, but also faraway places such as Terrassa and Montserrat. Within greater Barcelona, TMB travelcards and multi-trip tickets are valid for travel.

BY TAXI

Taxis are black with a yellow stripe and can be hailed on the street, found at ranks or ordered by phone. The basic fare tariff applies from 6.00-22.00 Mon-Fri, with slightly higher rates from 22.00-6.00 and on Sat, Sun and PH. There are supplements for each piece of luggage carried in the boot and trips to and from the airport and train stations. Details of these and other supplements are shown on an information panel on the side window of taxis, and it is worth checking that you are not being overcharged.

A receipt is un *recibo/un rebut*. If you want to make a complaint, make sure you get a properly-completed receipt and call the municipal helpline on *T* 010. It is usual (but not obligatory) to tip about 10 per cent.

Barnataxi, *T* 933 577 755

Taxi Radiomòbil, *T* 933 581 111

Radio Taxi, *T* 932 250 000

All of these taxi companies have cabs adapted for people in wheelchairs, or call for *T* 934 208 088 for specialist service.

MUSEUM PASSES

The **Articket**, available from tourist offices and participating museums, costs approx. €16 and includes entrance to the Museu Nacional d'Art de Catalunya (MNAC), Museu d'Art Modern, Fundació Joan Miró, Fundació Antoni Tàpies, Museu d'Art Contemporani de Barcelona (MACBA), Centre de Cultura Contemporània de Barcelona (CCCB) and La Pedrera. If you visit all these museums, the saving is around 40 per cent on individual entrance prices. The Articket is valid for three months.

The **Modernisme Route** (Ruta del Modernisme; available from Centre del Modernisme, Casa Amatller, Passeig de Gràcia 41, *T* 934 880 139) costs €3 and comprises an informative book (available in English) and vouchers giving free entrance or discounts at the museums and buildings along the route, which include the Palau Güell, Palau de la Música Catalana, La Pedrera and the Sagrada Família. Discounts of 30-50 per cent are also available with the **Barcelona Card** and with **Tourist Bus** vouchers, details of which are given on p 163 and p 168.

For up to date information on exhibitions, buy the weekly listings magazine *Guía del Ocio*, or visit their website, www.guiadelocio.com. Also useful is the quarterly *Museums of Barcelona* booklet, which is available for €1 from museum shops.

OTHER ESSENTIALS
DISABLED TRAVELLERS

The city is making a huge effort to improve conditions for people with disabilities, but there is a long way to go. As a rule of thumb, anything built or modified since 1992 is accessible to people with physical disabilities and people using wheelchairs. The whole Vila Olímpica area, for example, is wheelchair-friendly, with easy access to the beaches, promenades and marina. Places that are totally accessible with above-average facilities include the MACBA Contemporary Art Museum, the Liceu opera house, the Auditori concert hall and the Icària Yelmo multiplex cinema, which shows films in the original version with subtitles.

For information on public transport, see the Getting Around section above or contact **SIPTRE**, a helpline for people with mobility problems that publishes a guide to transport services and answers specific transport queries (*T* 934 860 752). The general city helpline (*T* 010 from Barcelona, *T* 906 427 017 from elsewhere) is a good starting point for all sorts of mobility and accessibility queries. The **Institut Municipal de Persones Amb Disminució** (Av. Diagonal 233, *T* 934 132 775) is dedicated to improving facilities in

Barcelona, and publishes a very useful map, the Plano de la Barcelona Accesible, which shows accessibility at tourist sights, public transport etc.

In the UK, information can be obtained from the Spanish Tourist Office and also from the **Royal Association for Disability and Rehabilitation** (RADAR) at 12 City Forum, 250 City Road, London EC1V 8AF (**T** 020 7250 3222, www.radar.org.uk) and **Holiday Care Services**, 2nd Floor, Imperial Buildings, Victoria Road, Horley, Surrey R6 7PZ (**T** 01293 774 535).

In the US from **Mobility International USA**, PO Box 10767, www.miusa.org and **Society for Accessible Travel and Hospitality**, 347 Fifth Ave, Suite 610, NY 10016, **T** 212 725 8253, www.sath.org.

CONSULATES

Australia, Gran Via Carles III 98, **T** 933 309 496

Canada, C/Elisenda de Pinós 10, **T** 932 042 700

Ireland, Gran Via Carles III 94, **T** 934 915 021

Netherlands, Av. Diagonal 601, **T** 934 106 210

New Zealand, Travessera de Gràcia 64, **T** 932 090 399

UK, Torre Barcelona, Av. Diagonal 477, **T** 933 666 620

USA, Passeig de la Reina Elisenda 23-25, **T** 932 802 227

EMERGENCIES

Emergency Services **T** 112

National Police **T** 091

Barcelona Police **T** 092

Fire brigade **T** 080

Ambulance **T** 061

Tourist Assistance Police Station, La Rambla 43, **T** 933 441 300

HEALTH
MEDICAL SERVICES

Treatment is provided free to EU citizens with an E111 form at the Accident & Emergency (Urgències) department of state-run hospitals. Go to one of the following:

Hospital Clínic, C/Villaroel 170, **T** 932 275 400 in the Eixample, which has an adjacent first-aid centre at C/València 184.

Centre d'Urgències Perecamps, Av. Drassanes 13-15, **T** 934 410 600 at the bottom of La Rambla.

Hospital del Mar, Passeig Marítim 25-29, **T** 932 483 000 by the beach between Barceloneta and the Port Olímpic.

LATE-NIGHT CHEMISTS
There is a rota system for late-night and weekend opening (*farmàcie de guàrdia*), which is shown in pharmacy windows and listed in newspapers or is available by calling **T** 010.

Farmàcia Clapés, La Rambla 98, **T** 933 012 843, open 24 hours

Farmàca Alvarez, Passeig de Gràcia 26, **T** 933 021 124, open 24 hours

LOST OR STOLEN PROPERTY
If your passport or valuables are lost or stolen, report it at the Tourist Assistance police station at La Rambla 43, **T** 933 441 300. This process known as a *denuncia* and is necessary for insurance purposes.

Municipal Lost Property Office (Servie de Troballes), City Hall, C/Ciutat 9, **T** 934 023 161 or **T** 010.

Credit card companies:

Visa	**T** 900 974 445
Mastercard	**T** 900 971 231
American Express	**T** 915 720 303 or **T** 902 375 637
Diners Club	**T** 915 474 000

OPENING HOURS
Most shops open Mon-Sat 9.00/10.00-13.30/14.00 and 16.30/17.00-20.00/21.00. Many shops in the centre, department stores and shopping centres do not close at lunchtime. Small shops may close Saturday afternoon.

Banks are open Mon-Fri 8.30-14.00, with main branches opening until 16.00/17.00. Most banks open Sat 8.30-12.00/13.00.

PUBLIC HOLIDAYS

1 January	New Year's Day
6 January	Epiphany
Easter	Good Friday, Easter Sunday and Easter Monday (movable)
1 May	Labour Day
Whit Monday	(movable)
24 June	St John's Day. Fireworks and bonfires the night before
15 August	Assumption
11 September	La Diada. Catalan National Day
24 September	Mercè, patron saint of Barcelona. City holiday preceding a week of festivities
12 October	Columbus Day. The Feast of the Spanish-speaking nations
1 November	All Saints' Day
6 December	Constitution Day
8 December	Immaculate Conception
25 December	Christmas Day
26 December	Boxing Day

The festival of St George (*Sant Jordi*), the patron saint of Catalunya, on 23 April, when it is customary to exchange a book and a rose as a sign of love and friendship, is not a public holiday, and all shops and museums are open that day.

SIGHTSEEING TOURS
BY COACH

Tourist Bus (Bus Turístic), 1 or 2 day (€16 or €20) hop-on-hop-off ticket. There are two routes in open-topped buses around the city, passing all the major points of interest. Every ten minutes in summer, slightly less frequently at other times of year. Discounts at all the museums and attractions along the route. Tickets available on the bus or at tourist offices. *T* 010 or *T* 906 301 282

Barcelona Tours, 1 or 2 day (€17 or €21) hop-on-hop-off tickets for tours in open-topped buses, *T* 933 176 454

BY BIKE

Un Cotxe Menys, C/Esparteria 3, *T* 932 682 015,
www.bicicletabarcelona.com. Tours on Sat and Sun leaving at 10.00,
€20 including bike

Trixi Tour, *T* 934 555 887, www.trixi.info. Tricycle taxis along the
waterfront. Start from end of Ramblas, Port Vell or flag one down
on the promenade. €10 for 30 minutes, or €1.50 per kilometre

The **Barna bici map**, available from tourist offices, shows cycle routes
around the city. Information *T* 934 027 504, www.bcn.es/bicicleta

BY BOAT

Les Golondrines, Plaça Portal de la Pau, Moll de Drassanes,
T 934 423 106, www.lasgolondrinas.com. Trips around the harbour
and along to the Port Olímpic.

WALKING

Barcelona Walking Tours, Gothic Quarter or Picasso's Barcelona. Sat and
Sun from Plaça de Catalunya tourist office. €7, *T* 906 301 282,
www.barcelonaturisme.com.

PLACES TO STAY

Tourist accommodation in the city is at a premium throughout the
year, and in 2004 will be in particular demand because of the
Univeral Forum of Cultures (p 173). Visitors are advised to book
rooms as far in advance as possible.

All hotels are officially classified, but prices and standards vary
considerably, and classification does not take décor or style into
account. A *hostal* is a no-frills hotel. The price bands quoted here
are for a double room with ensuite bath or shower. Useful
websites include www.hostelworld.com, www.barcelona-on-
line.es and www.1st-barcelona-hotels.com.

€ €50–€100

€€ €100–€150

€€€ €150 upwards

HOTELS
GAUDÍ AND THE EIXAMPLE

€   **Central**, C/Diputació 346, *T* 932 451 981. Characterful *hostal* located in Modernista building with mosaic floors. 13 rooms, all different. From €60. *M* Tetuán

D'Uxelles, Gran Via 688 and 667, *T* 932 652 560, www.hotelduxelles.com. Romantic and pretty, the 14 rooms are painted pastel colours with rustic antiques and canopies over the beds. Some rooms have terraces. From €80. *M* Tetuán

Ginebra, Rambla de Catalunya 1, *T* 933 171 063. 12 rooms on the third floor of an impressive building overlooking Plaça de Catalunya. Ask for one with a view. Family-run with good bathrooms. From €65. *M* Catalunya

Girona, C/Girona 24, *T* 932 650 259, www.hostalgirona.com. Characterful *hostal* in 19c building with lots of original features including mosaic floors and Modernista furniture. New bathrooms. €60. *M* Urquinaona

Qué Tal, C/Mallorca 290, *T* 934 592 366. Gay-run *hostal* in Modernista building. 14 brightly-painted rooms with original floor and ceilings. The Italian owners are happy to help you plan your stay. From €80. *M* Verdaguer, Passeig de Gràcia

Windsor, Rambla de Catalunya 84, *T* 932 151 198. 15 ensuite rooms in Modernista building. Good location for sightseeing, shopping and cafés. From €65. *M* Passeig de Gràcia

€€   **Actual**, C/Rosselló 238, *T* 935 520 550, www.hotelactual.com. Elegant contemporary design in natural tones. Opened in 2002. 29 rooms, some with views of La Pedrera. €140. *M* Diagonal

Gran Via, Gran Vía de les Corts Catalanes 642, *T* 933 181 900, www.nnhotels.es. Lots of old-world charm in palatial building near Passeig de Gràcia. Roof terrace. 53 rooms. €120. *M* Passeig de Gràcia

€€€ **Claris**, C/Pau Claris 150, *T* 934 876 262, www.derbyhotels.es. 19c mansion converted into designer hotel. Near Gaudí buildings and shops. Rooftop pool. From €360. *M* Passeig de Gràcia

La Florida, Carretera Vallvidrera al Tibidabo 83-93, *T* 932 593 000, www.hotellaflorida.com. Lavishly revamped hotel on Tibidabo hill with views across the city. Suites by top designers and state-of-the-art spa. From €320. Shuttle bus service to centre

Omm, C/Rosselló 179, **T** 934 877 672, www.grupotragaluz.com. Designed by Juli Capella and opened at the end of 2003, this is the first hotel from the highly successful Tragaluz restaurant group. Near La Pedrera. From approx. €180. **M** Diagonal

Prestige, Passeig de Gràcia 62, **T** 932 724 180, www.prestigepaseodegracia.com. Hip minimalist hotel near Gaudí's La Pedrera and Casa Batlló, as well as shops and restaurants. Favourite of fashion and media crowd. From €175. **M** Passeig de Gràcia

Regente, Rambla de Catalunya 76, **T** 934 875 989, www.hcchotels.com. Modernista building by Evarist Juncosa in handy location. Comfortable, good service. Top floor rooms have terraces with great views. Rooftop pool. From €232. **M** Passeig de Gràcia

PICASSO MUSEUM AND THE RIBERA

€ **Francia**, C/Rera Palau 4, **T** 933 190 376. In the heart of the medieval Born area, the 20 rooms in this hostal are pleasant and comfortable, but not all ensuite. From €45. **M** Barceloneta

Pensio 2000, C/Sant Pere Més Alt 6, **T** 933 107 466, www.pensio2000.com. Seven large rooms, on first floor (no lift) opposite the Modernista Palau de la Mùsica. More like a large apartment than a hotel. Good breakfast. €60. **M** Urquinaona

Orleans, Av. Marquès de l'Argentera 13, **T** 933 197 382. Surprisingly smart rooms on 1st floor of apartment block near Born area and seafront. No lift. From €50. **M** Barceloneta

€€ **Banys Orientals**, C/Argenteria 37, **T** 932 688 460, www.hotelbanysorientals.com. Astonishingly good value, this comfortable minimalist hotel in the hip Born area is decorated in soft grey and mauve tones. €102. **M** Jaume I

Nouvel, C/Santa Ana 18-20, **T** 933 018 274, www.hotelnouvel.com. Refurbished Modernista building with wrought-iron balconies and carved stone façade. Just off the Ramblas near Plaça de Catalunya. 54 rooms. From €110. **M** Catalunya

Park, Avda Marquès de Argentera 11, **T** 933 196 000. Stylish hotel with distinctive '50s architecture. In Born district near waterfront. Excellent restaurant. From €120. **M** Barceloneta

Urquinaona, Ronda de Sant Pere 24, **T** 932 681 336, www.barcelonahotel.com/urquinaona. Well-designed, comfortable rooms with above average facilities, €102. **M** Urquinaona

€€€ **Arts**, C/Marina 19-21, *T* 932 211 000,
www.ritzcarlton.com/hotels/barcelona. This 45-storey skyscraper
overlooking the Port Olímpic marina is one of Barcelona's
signature contemporary buildings and is celebrating its 10th
anniversary in 2004. A favourite with celebrities. Outdoor pool.
From €360 (also special packages). *M* Ciutadella Vila Olímpica

MACBA AND THE RAVAL

€ **Cèntric**, C/Casanova 13, *T* 934 267 573, www.hostalcentric.com.
Comfortable *hostal* with above average decoration and facilities.
From €82. *M* Universitat

Gat Raval, C/Joaquín Costa 44, *T* 934 816 670. Well-designed in
crisp green and white, this is the first of a new kind of no-frills
hotel by an enterprising young team. Near MACBA. Internet access
and nightlife information. No lift. Gat Xino is scheduled to open
nearby in 2004. From €70. *M* Universitat

Grau, C/Ramelleres 27, *T* 933 018 135, www.hostalgrau.com.
Friendly family-run *hostal* in handy location. Apartments available
on top floor. Good breakfast served in cosy café. From €60.
M Catalunya

Peninsular, C/Sant Pau 34, *T* 933 023 138. Formerly a convent, the
Peninsular has basic rooms set around an airy courtyard filled with
plants and contemporary art. Breakfast served in attractive room.
€80. *M* Liceu

Ramos, C/Hospital 36, *T* 933 020 723. Good budget choice in
convenient location off Ramblas. Rooms, on 1st and 2nd floors, are
set around a courtyard and all have bathrooms. Front rooms
overlook Plaça de Sant Agustí. No lift. From €60. *M* Liceu

€€ **Mesón Castilla**, C/Valldoncella 5, *T* 933 182 182,
www.mesoncastilla.com. The two-star rating undervalues this
charming hotel with good facilities and lots of character. Near
Plaça de Catalunya and MACBA museum. 56 rooms, some with
terraces. Family rooms available. From €120. *M* Universitat

Millenni, Ronda de Sant Pau 14, *T* 934 414 177,
www.hotelmillennium.com. 19c building converted into stylish
hotel in 2001. On edge of Raval district and near Montjuïc. Wireless
internet access. From €130. *M* Paral.lel

Sant Agustí, Plaça Sant Agustí 3, *T* 933 181 658, www.hotelsa.com.
Contemporary and traditional design go well together in this
converted 18c convent just off the Ramblas. Some rooms have

balconies overlooking the square, but attic rooms have the most character. Good breakfast. Free internet access. 77 rooms. From €130. *M* Liceu

MONTJUÏC

€ **Nuevo Triunfo**, C/Cabanes 24, *T* 934 425 933. At the bottom of Montjuïc hill, rooms are basic but clean and comfortable. Some have terraces. Friendly, helpful staff. Also handy for Raval area. From €90. *M* Paral.lel

€€ **Paral.lel**, C/Poeta Cabanyes 5-7, *T* 933 291 104, www.nnhotels.es. Comfortable place in residential street a short walk from the centre. €110. *M* Paral.lel

€€€ **Miramar**, Av. Miramar, *T* 934 521 432, www.thesteingroup.com. Opening in 2004, the Miramar is a luxury conversion of a former grand hotel on Montjuïc hill with spectacular views across the city and seafront. From approx. €280. *M* Espanya

ART CALENDAR

APRIL

Primavera Fotografica 2004, photography exhibitions at various venues, organized by the Institut de Cultura de Barcelona. *T* 933 017 775, www.bcn.es

The Universal Forum of Cultures, Barcelona 2004

From 9 May to 26 September 2004 Barcelona will host the fourth great exhibition of its modern history, the Universal Forum of Cultures. A celebration the diversity of global culture, the Forum will include a summer-long programme of concerts, dance, art and museum exhibitions drawn from around the world.

Many of the exhibits and events will be held in @22, an urban development of office buildings, residences, exhibition spaces and parks that transformed part of the run-down northern industrial neighbourhood of Sant Adrià de Besòs. The city centre's concert halls, museums and public squares will also be used.

The opening ceremonies, to be held on 9 May, will feature a pyrotechnic spectacle of 28 tonnes of fireworks launched to music by composers from five continents, accompanied by a choreographed display involving dozens of small craft along 3km of coast. The show will be repeated for the closing ceremonies on 26 September.

Many events will be free. Tickets for events for which there is a charge are sold on a one-day, three-day, or season-long basis; ticket prices will increase towards summer, but the initial prices are set at €17.90, €35.70, €142.80 respectively. For more information on this historical event consult www.barcelona2004.org.

Brian A. Catlos

MAY
Artexpo, Annual art fair at Fira de Barcelona

JUNE
Sonar, International Festival of Advanced Music and Multimedia Art at Centre de Cultura Contemporània de Barcelona (CCCB), MACBA and other venues. *T* 934 422 972, www.sonar.es. Mid June

JULY
Grec, theatre, dance and music festival. *T* 933 017 775, www.grec.bcn.es. Throughout July

SEPTEMBER
Festes de la Mercè, city festival with art events around the city. Week around September 24. *T* 933 017 775, www.bcn.es

OCTOBER
Gran Teatre del Liceu, start of opera, concerts and recitals season at the Gran Teatre del Liceu. *T* 934 859 900, www.liceubarcelona.com

art glossary

Barceló i Artigues, Miquel (b. 1957) Mallorcan-born painter now based in Barcelona. His influences have included Klee, Art Brut, the Surrealists and Jackson Pollock. He joined the Taller Llunàtic group, taking part in their happenings, and was involved with their publication, *Néon de Suro*.

Berenguer Mestres, Francesc (1866-1914) Architect and designer who worked with Gaudí on many of his buildings.

Borrassà, Lluís (d. 1424/6) Member of a family of painters from Girona. His best known attributed works include Set Goigs de la Mare de Déu (1402), the chapel of St Anthony in Manresa Cathedral (1410), and the retables of St Peter of Ègara in Terrassa (1411) and the Convent of St Claire in Vic (1415). His work represents Catalan International Gothic, a style which blended Italian, French and Flemish influences.

Brossa, Joan (1919-98) Influential conceptual artist, poet and playwright. Brossa was a founding member of Dau al Set collective (1948) along with Antoni Tàpies. In 1960 he had a collaborative exhibition with Joan Miró (Poets, Painters, Sculptors) and another with Tàpies in 1980 (One is No One). He has become best known as a poet (e.g. 'This Made Me Joan Brossa', 1950) and has strived to combine poetry and drama with visual arts.

Calatrava, Santiago (b. 1951) Valencian architect and engineer. The creator of ground-breaking projects across Spain and Europe, Calatrava designed Barcelona's Bac de Roda bridge and the communications tower in the Olympic complex.

Casas i Carbó, Ramon (1866-1932) Like many contemporary Catalan painters, Casas installed himself in Montmartre, Paris, in the 1880s and came under the influence of Toulouse-Lautrec. By 1897 he was back in Barcelona where he co-founded the Modernista haunt Els Quatre Gats (p 84), and two years later launched a review of the same name. He is best known for his posters and his portraits of contemporary cultural and political figures, including Alfonso XIII.

Cerdà, Ildefons (1815–76) This Catalan engineer and urbanist was commissioned in 1859, amidst much controversy, to plan Barcelona's new town, or Eixample (meaning expansion), which carried the city beyond the limits of the medieval walls and incorporated surrounding villages. His rationalist plan called for a grid made up of regular blocks (*illas* or *manzanas*) of shops and flats, each with an open-air public garden in the centre. The grid was cut across by two streets following a latitudinal (La Meridiana) and longitudinal (La Diagonal) avenue. In 1873–4 he served as president of the city council.

Chillida, Eduardo (b. 1924) Basque sculptor inspired by the work of Pau Gargallo and known for his expressive if austere works of iron and wood. Winner of national and international awards, examples of his work can be seen in the Barcelona Prat Airport and the Parc de la Ciutadella.

Cubism An artistic style first developed by Pablo Picasso and Georges Braque between 1907 and 1914, which represented an analytical approach to form and colour by depicting an object from several viewpoints. It was also profoundly influenced by so-called Primitive art. The seminal work was Picasso's *Les Desmoiselles d' Avignon* (1907; MoMA, New York). Cubism was more than a style of painting, it was a cultural movement which had an impact on literature, architecture, music and drama.

Domènech i Montaner, Lluís (1850–1923) A key figure of Modernisme, this architect, historian and politician studied in both Barcelona and Madrid. His first great public works were the Castle of the Three Dragons and Hotel International, built for the 1888 Universal Exhibition. More commissions followed, including the Editorial Montaner i Simón, Casa Lleó Morera, Hospital de Sant Pau and Palau de la Música Catalana. Domènech i Montaner was a committed Catalanist; his architecture drew strongly from the Romanesque and Gothic styles, typified by flights of fantasy such as 'medieval' turrets – a trademark feature.

Fortuny i Marsal, Marià (1838-74) A native of Reus and graduate of the Llotja art school in Barcelona, Fortuny was a painter and engraver. He was became an establishment figure who in 1859 was appointed official painter of the African campaign. He was acclaimed by contemporaries for his subtle realism.

Gaudí i Cornet, Antoni (1852-1926) Antoni Gaudí is the most famous and influential of the Modernista architects. He was also a master craftsman; his skills included ironwork, woodwork, glass-making and ceramics. Born in Reus, his professional life centred strongly on Barcelona. Here, under the patronage of the wealthy Güell family, he carried out some of his most famous commissions, including Palau Güell (1885-90) and Park Güell (1900-14). Other notable buildings include Casa Batlló and La Pedrera. He borrowed freely from Gothic, Romanesque, Moorish and Mudéjar architectural styles, adding important technical innovations and developing a unique organic style of design. In later life he dedicated himself exclusively to the Sagrada Família (begun in 1883). A passionate Catholic, Gaudí became so immersed in his work at the church that when he was struck down by a tram passers-by thought him an indigent. There is a strong movement to sanctify Gaudí, and the architect is likely to be beatified soon.

Gothic The dominant artistic and architectural style of Western Europe between the 13c and 15c, revived internationally as neo-Gothic in the 19c. In architecture it is characterized by the ogival or pointed arch, and its exaltation of light and verticality over the mass and weight of Romanesque. The determination to increase the window area of exterior walls prompted engineering innovations, including the development of external supports known as flying buttresses. Catalan Gothic was more sober and restrained than the French and Italian versions of the style, and retained a strong Romanesque influence. The Cathedral of Barcelona (begun 1298) is typical, while Santa María del Mar (1329-79) is a particularly beautiful example of Catalan Gothic architecture. In painting and sculpture Gothic emphasized naturalistic detail and accurate anatomy in figures, but the rules of perspective were not rigorously employed. Major figures of Catalan Gothic painting include **Ferrer Bassa** (early 14c), **Bernat Martorell** (early 15c), **Lluís Dalmau** (late 15c) and **Jaume Huguet** (late 15c). Examples of their work can be seen in the National Museum of Catalan Art (MNAC).

Güell i Bacigalupi, Eusebi (1846-1918) This entrepreneur and industrialist epitomized the Catalan upper-middle class which was behind the Modernista movement. The son of an industrialist, Eusebi opened his own cloth factory (alongside which Colònia Güell would be built in 1891) and cement business and acquired interests in his wife's family's businesses, which included a bank, tobacco company and railway. A committed Catalanist, he was politically active as a city counsellor, provincial deputy and senator. In 1918 he was named Count of Güell. He is remembered now as Gaudí's great patron.

Homar i Mezquida, Gaspar (1870-1953) An important figure in Modernista decorative arts, a master of many media including metal, wood, textiles and ceramics. He believed that the objects and furniture of daily life could be designed as works of art. The interior of the Casa Lleó Morera was his most important commission.

Huguet, Jaume (c 1415-92) Gothic painter strongly influenced by Bernat Martorell and Lluís Dalmau. His workshop produced a series of masterful retables from the mid-1450s to mid-1460s. Many of these are exhibited at the MNAC (p 133), including the *retables of St Vincent* (1455-8) and *St Michael* (1455-60). Later works, such as his painting of *St Augustine* (1465-80), also at the MNAC, show the influence of the Italian Renaissance. His work is characterized by a strong interest in naturalistic detail, particularly in his character studies, as well as impressive use of colour.

Jujol Gibert, Josep Maria (1879-1949) Architect who worked with Gaudí on a number of projects, including the Park Güell and La Pedrera. He specialized in tile and wrought-iron decoration.

Llimona i Burgeura, Josep (1864-1934) Important Modernista sculptor, who trained at the Llotja art school (where Picasso's father would later teach). Along with his brother Joan, a notable painter, he founded the Cercle Artístic de Sant Lluc, a strongly Catholic Modernista collective. He worked on a number of public projects including the *Columbus Monument* (1886), at Plaça Portal de la Pau, and the Universal Exhibition of 1888.

Mariscal, Xavier (b. 1950) Francesc Xavier Errando Mariscal cut his teeth as a graphic artist in the Barcelona underground movement during the late Franco era and went on to become one of the city's favourite designers. He has worked on diverse decorative and design projects including bars, restaurants and clubs, and is most noted for designing Cobi and Petra, the cartoon mascots of the 1992 Olympic and Para-Olympic Games.

Meier, Richard (b. 1934) American architect who designed the MACBA (p 93). His buildings include the Getty Center in Los Angeles and the Frankfurt Museum for Decorative Arts. His many awards include the Pritzker Prize in 1984.

Mendoza, Eduardo (b. 1943) Barcelona-born writer now residing in New York whose best known novel, *City of Marvels* (the subject of a film) is set in Barcelona during the Modernista age.

Mir i Trinxet, Joaquim (1873-1940) Barcelona-born painter, most famous for his Catalan and Mallorcan landscapes. Began his career with a luminous naturalism related to Fauvism, which became increasingly exuberant and abstract as he matured. He was commissioned in 1927 to paint the great mural in the palace of the Generalitat.

Miró i Ferrà, Joan (1893-1983) Barcelona's greatest native artist, this painter and sculptor has profoundly influenced succeeding generations. His early work, which was first shown at the Dalmau Galleries, was clearly expressionist although influenced by Cubism and Fauvism. In 1919 he made the obligatory shift to Paris, which together with Mallorca became his main residence. The following decade saw him move towards more abstract, Surrealist influenced work, including sculptures incorporating 'ready made' elements, which he called 'constructions'. The horror of the Civil War forced him to reappraise his artistic language, and it was in the late 1930s that his recognizable style emerged, typified by symbols of birds, women and celestial bodies. In Barcelona his works can be seen in the Fundació Joan Miró as well as in the Parc del Excorxador and on La Ramblas.

Modernisme A widespread cultural movement of the last decades of the 19c and first of the 20c, known elsewhere as Art Nouveau,

Modern Style, Jugendstil, Stile Liberty, Sezessionstil, Style 1900 and Style Nouille. It is a style which emphasizes decorative elements and was initially inspired by the Arts and Crafts movement in England and by the work of Symbolist artists. As an architectural style it is the hallmark of Barcelona, thanks to Gaudí, Domènech i Montaner and Puig i Cadalfach. Notable Catalan Modernista painters include Casas i Rusiñol and Joan Llimona, while the most famous sculptors are **Josep Llimona**, **Eusebi Arnau** and **Pau Gargallo**. The 1900 Paris Exhibition was its crowning moment; subsequently it began to decline, although it influenced young artists such as Miró, Picasso and Nonell. It is less well known but also important as a literary movement, best represented in Catalonia by the poems of Maragall. Catalan Modernisme was very much tied to the nationalist aspirations of the region's wealthy new industrial class; it was given its name as a disdainful dismissal by its early critics.

Mudéjar The style of the architecture and craft of the Muslims who remained in Spain under Christian rule until they were expelled from Aragon, Catalonia and Valencia in 1607. The key manifestations include brickwork, cabinetwork and ceramics. Mudéjar brickwork, most common in Aragon, features elaborate geometric patterns on the exterior walls, often interspersed with ceramic decoration. Mudéjars were renowned for their skills in carpentry, and were commissioned to create elaborate artesonado ceilings. They were also responsible for the Valencian ceramic industry, and Muslim styles and sensibilities are evident in much peninsular pottery. Neo-Mudéjar represents a late-19c revival of forms and styles based on Mudéjar craft.

Nonell i Monturiol, Isidre (1873-1911) A classmate of Llimona at the Llotja art school; like so many contemporaries Nonell went to Paris, where he exhibited at the 15th Exhibition of Impressionist and Symbolists (1897). His early influences were Daumier, Monet and Toulouse-Lautrec; from 1900 he concentrated on sketching society's outcasts, including the disabled and gypsies. His first local recognition came in 1910, and when he died unexpectedly a year later he became a cult figure. Aficionados debate whether the painting style known as *fregit* ('fried') was invented by him or his contemporary, and rival, Picasso.

Noucentisme This style, which succeeded Modernisme in Catalonia, was proclaimed as a movement in 1906 by the essayist and critic Eugeni d'Ors. While Modernisme was influenced by the medieval period, Noucentisme looked to rationalism inspired by the Classical world. Important in literature as well as in painting and sculpture, leading figures included Joaquim Sunyer and Enric Casanovas. In architecture, Puig i Cadalfach inspired several Noucentists, including Josep Goday and Rafael Masó. The transition to Noucentisme can be seen in buildings such as the Palau de Justicia, while the full-blown style dominates the exhibition grounds at Montjuïc, including the MNAC.

Plateresque This Spanish architectural style developed in the late 15c. It was a local derivative of the Renaissance style and featured elaborately decorated elements on doorways and window frames (made in the style of silver - *plata* - ware) set in plain walls.

Puig i Cadafalch, Josep (1867-1956) A leading Modernista architect, art historian and politician. He was apprenticed to Domènech i Montaner, whom he later came to rival in his achievements. His first Modernista creation was Casa Martí (Els Quatre Gats) in 1897. This was followed by Casa Amatller (1900), Casa Macaya (1901), Casa Serra (1907), Palau Quadras (1905) and Casa Terrades (1905). His style was eclectic, mixing Classical, Gothic, Romanesque and Moorish elements, although he showed a marked inclination for Germanic-style Gothic, which for him underlined Catalonia's connection to Europe, independent of Spain. Later works show a shift towards Noucentisme, although Casarramona (1924; now the Caixaforum) is still markedly Modernista. He was also involved in planning the Eixample district and renovations to the Old City, including the construction of the Via Laietana (1914) and the expansion of the Plaça de Catalunya (1923).

Renaissance Meaning rebirth or renewal, this wide-ranging cultural movement originated in 14c Italy and gradually spread throughout Western Europe, reviving the literary, artistic and architectural styles of the Classical past. It developed alongside the contemporary intellectual movement known as Humanism. In art, human subjects began to rival purely religious themes and the naturalistic tendencies of Gothic art were further developed with new elements of composition, including perspective, introduced. The Renaissance reached Catalonia in the late 14c and was the dominant artistic style by the middle of the next century, encouraged by Barcelona's political domination of Naples.

Renaixença Meaning 'renaissance' in Catalan, referring to the 'rebirth' of Catalan literary and intellectual culture in the mid-19c, coinciding with nationalist movements across Europe. Emphasis was placed on modernization and standardization of the Catalan language, the study of folklore and popular customs. In 1874, the medieval literary Olympics known as the Jocs Florals (Floral Games) was reinstituted by the city's leading art patrons.

Romanesque Artistic and architectural style drawing on Roman sources for inspiration, current in Catalonia between the early 11c and the 13c. In architecture, the basilica model was used for church plans. Churches of this period tend to be without external decoration, with the exception of the sculpted lintels of main doorways, and the often elaborately carved corbels and capitals (found particularly in cloisters). However, interiors were lavishly decorated with murals illustrating Old and New Testament themes. The most notable examples of Catalan Romanesque church architecture include the door of the abbey-church at Ripoll, and the Cathedral of Urgell, while in Barcelona the early 12c Sant Pau del Camp is a rare survival. Some of the vivid murals of the churches of the Pyrenees which escaped destruction can be found at the National Museum of Catalan Art (MNAC) and at the Museu Diocesà in Barcelona.

Rusiñol i Prats, Santiago (1861-1931) Modernista painter, author and playwright, and a co-founder of the Els Quatre Gats group. Although less well-known than his contemporaries, he is credited with introducing modern art to Catalonia in 1890.

Sert i Badia, Josep Maria (1874-1945) Painter and member of the Cercle Artístic de Sant Lluc. Known for his ecclesiastical and pacifist works, as well as for scenery design for the Ballets Russes. In the 1930s and '40s he was in great demand across Europe and America as a muralist.

Tàpies, Antoni (b. 1923) Barcelona native, regarded as Spain's greatest living artist and an important theorist and critic. A founding member of the Dau al Set collective (1948) influenced by Klee and Miró, by 1953 he had achieved transatlantic fame. Tàpies developed an idiosyncratic abstract style which exploits an inventive and original mixing of media including paint, cloth and metal. In the 1970s he became politically active against the fascist regime, initiating a phase of poster-making. He founded the Fundació Tàpies in 1987, which has become a major Barcelona art museum and resource centre, featuring the largest single collection of Tàpies' work and hosting exhibitions of contemporary artists from around the world.

Trencadís A decorative style (similar to mosaic) pioneered by Gaudí, which involves the fixing of ceramic shards (often re-used household items) on exterior and interior surfaces to create a patterned surface. It is much in evidence in Park Güell and La Pedrera.

Vázquez-Montalbán, Manuel (1939-2003). Barcelona novelist, critic and essayist who wrote in Castilian Spanish. He is most famous for his creation of Pepe Carvalho, a detective working in the seedy parts of Barcelona, who debuted in *I Killed Kennedy* (1962) and continued as the protagonist of a dozen novels, notably sharing his author's gastronomic passions. He received national and international prizes for some of his other works of fiction. His political essays locate him in the European Socialist tradition.

First edition 2004
Published by A&C Black Publishers Ltd
37 Soho Square, London W1D 3QZ

ISBN 0-7136-6693-5

Published in the United States of America by
WW Norton & Company, Inc
500 Fifth Avenue, New York, NY 10110

ISBN 0-393-32590-3

Published simultaneously in Canada by
Penguin Books Canada Limited
10 Alcorn Avenue, Ontario M4V 3B2

Series devised by Gemma Davies
Series designed by Jocelyn Lucas
Editorial and production: Gemma Davies, Jocelyn Lucas, Lilla Nwenu-Msimang, Miranda Robson, Kim Teo, Judy Tither

Maps by Mapping Company Ltd. Metro map kindly supplied by the Barcelona transport authority.

Photographic acknowledgements
Front cover and inside front cover: Stained-glass ceiling of the Palau de la Música Catalana, Barcelona, by Antoni Rigalt © Sylvain Grandadam, courtesy of Robert Harding Picture Library
Back cover: Ironwork gate in Park Güell, Barcelona, by Antoni Gaudí © Jocelyn Lucas
Inside: For permission to reproduce illustrations throughout the book, the publishers would like to thank the following: CaixaForum (p 141), Centre de Cultura Contemporània (p 98); Lisa Hirst (pp 8, 11, 12, 14, 19, 24, 25, 29, 30, 31, 32, 37, 38, 39, 43, 44, 77, 80, 82, 103, 105, 107, 115); Jocelyn Lucas (p 22); The Museum of Contemporary Art, Barcelona (p 95); Spanish Tourist Office (pp 21, 23, 33, 35, 69, 70, 71, 74, 76, 89, 99, 119)

Printed and bound in Singapore by Tien Wah Press (Pte.) Ltd

KEY MAP TO ATLAS SECTION

Gaudí & the Eixample

Picasso Museum & the Ribera

MACBA & the Raval

Montjuïc

Ⓜ Metro Station

RENFE Renfe Station

F.G.C Ferrocarrils de la
Generalitat d Catalunya

ⓅⓄ Post Office

ⓘ Tourist Information

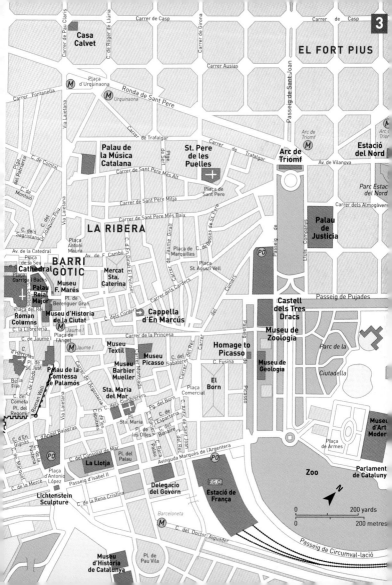

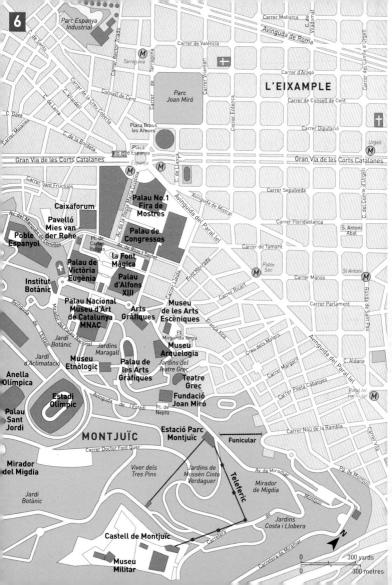

Parc Espanya Industrial

Carrer Mallorca

C. de Viladomat

Avinguda de Roma

Carrer de València

C. de Sants

Carrer Rector Triadó

Tarragona

Carrer de tarragona

Carrer Viamari

Carrer d'Aragó

L'EIXAMPLE

Carrer de la Creu Coberta

Consell de Cent

Carrer de Consell de Cent

C. Vilardell

C. Leiva

C. de Leiva

C. Gava

Carrer Moianes

C. de la Bordeta

Parc Joan Miró

Carrer Enlaça

Carrer Diputació

Urgell

F.G.C. d'Espanya

Plaça Braus les Arenes

Plaça d'Espanya

Gran Via de les Corts Catalanes

Espanya

Gran Via de les Corts Catalanes

Carrer Sant Fructuos

C. de Llança

Carrer Sepulveda

C. del Comte de Urgell

S. Antoni Abat

Av. del Marquès de Comillas

Caixaforum

Palau No.1 Fira de Mostres

Avinguda de Mistral

Carrer Floridablanca

Carrer de Tamarit

Pavelló Mies van der Rohe

Poble Espanyol

Pl. de Carles Buïgas

Av. de la Reina Maria Cristina

Palau de Congressos

Avinguda del Paral·lel

Carrer Ricart

Poble Sec

Carrer Manso

St Antoni

Av. de Rius i Taulet

la Font Màgica

Palau de Victòria Eugènia

Palau d'Alfons XIII

Font Honrada

Carrer Lleida

Carrer Parlament

Institut Botànic

Avinguda de l'Estadi

Mirador del Palau Nacional

Palau Nacional Museu d'Art de Catalunya MNAC

Arts Gràfiques

Museu de les Arts Escèniques

França Xica

Ronda de Sant Pau

Jardí Botànic

Jardins Maragall

Mirabda Xirgu

Museu Arqueologia

Creu dels Molers

Jardí d'Aclimatació

Museu Etnològic

Palau de les Arts Gràfiques

Jardins del Teatre Grec

Jardins dels Molers

Carrer Margarit

Avinguda del Paral·lel

C. Aldana

Anella Olímpica

Estadi Olímpic

Avinguda de l'Estadi

Teatre Grec

Fundació Joan Miró

Carrer Poeta Cabanyes

Parc·lel Funicular

Palau Sant Jordi

Pl. de Neptú

Carrer Nou de la Rambla

Carrer Vila

MONTJUÏC

Carrer Doctor Font Quer

Estació Parc Montjuïc

Funicular

Pg. de Montjuïc

Mirador del Migdia

Viver dels Tres Pins

Jardins de Mossèn Cinto Verdaguer

Av. de Miramar

Telefèric

Mirador de Migdia

Montjuïc

Jardí Botànic

Jardins Costa i Llobera

Castell de Montjuïc

Carretera

Carretera de Miramar

Museu Militar

N

| 0 | | 300 yards |
| 0 | | 300 metres |

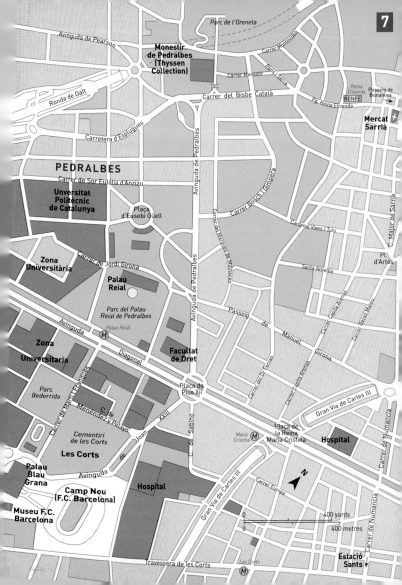

Parc de l'Oreneta

Avinguda de Pearson

Monestir de Pedralbes (Thyssen Collection)

Carrer Monterols

Carrer Montevideo

Pons i Serra

Carrer Monestir

Reina Elisenda

Passeig de Bonanova

Pg. Reina Elisenda

RENFE

Carrer del Bisbe Català

Ronda de Dalt

Carretera d'Esplugues

Mercat Sarrià

PEDRALBES

Carrer de Sor Eulàlia d'Anzizu

Avinguda de Pedralbes

Unversitat Politècnic de Catalunya

Carrer Bosch i Gimpera

Cardenal Vives i Tutó

Plaça d'Eusebi Güell

Carrer del Marquès de Mulhacén

Zona Universitària

Carrer de Jordi Girona

Santa Amelia

Pl. d'Artès

C. Major de Sarrià

Palau Reial

Parc del Palau Reial de Pedralbes

Passeig

de

Manuel

Girona

Carrer Capità Arenas

Carrer Benet Mateu

Ⓜ Palau Reial

Avinguda

Diagonal

Zona Universitaria

Facultat de Dret

Carrer de Capità Arenas

Gran Via de Carles III

Carrer de Numància

Parc Bederrida

Carrer de Martí i Franquès

Menéndez y Pelayo

C. de

XIII

Joan

de

Sabino

C.

Carrer del Dr Ferran

Plaça de Pius XII

Carrer Capità Arenas

Maria Cristina Ⓜ

Plaça de la Reina Maria Cristina

Hospital

Cementiri de les Corts

Les Corts

Palau Blau Grana

Avinguda

Camp Nou (F.C. Barcelona)

Hospital

Gran Via de Carles III

Carrer Europa

Museu F.C. Barcelona

N

0 ___ 400 yards

0 ___ 400 metres

Travessera de les Corts

Les Corts Ⓜ

Estació Sants ▼

art / shop / eat

art / shop / eat
FLORENCE

art / shop / eat
LONDON

art / shop / eat
NEW YORK

art / shop / eat
PARIS

art / shop / eat
ROME